# Environmentally Harmful Subsidies

## Policy Issues and Challenges

OECD

ORGANISATION FOR ECONOMIC CO-OPERATION AND DEVELOPMENT

# ORGANISATION FOR ECONOMIC CO-OPERATION AND DEVELOPMENT

Pursuant to Article 1 of the Convention signed in Paris on 14th December 1960, and which came into force on 30th September 1961, the Organisation for Economic Co-operation and Development (OECD) shall promote policies designed:
- to achieve the highest sustainable economic growth and employment and a rising standard of living in member countries, while maintaining financial stability, and thus to contribute to the development of the world economy;
- to contribute to sound economic expansion in member as well as non-member countries in the process of economic development; and
- to contribute to the expansion of world trade on a multilateral, non-discriminatory basis in accordance with international obligations.

The original member countries of the OECD are Austria, Belgium, Canada, Denmark, France, Germany, Greece, Iceland, Ireland, Italy, Luxembourg, the Netherlands, Norway, Portugal, Spain, Sweden, Switzerland, Turkey, the United Kingdom and the United States. The following countries became members subsequently through accession at the dates indicated hereafter: Japan (28th April 1964), Finland (28th January 1969), Australia (7th June 1971), New Zealand (29th May 1973), Mexico (18th May 1994), the Czech Republic (21st December 1995), Hungary (7th May 1996), Poland (22nd November 1996), Korea (12th December 1996) and the Slovak Republic (14th December 2000). The Commission of the European Communities takes part in the work of the OECD (Article 13 of the OECD Convention).

# FOREWORD

In 2001, OECD Ministers asked the Organisation to continue to assist them in formulating and implementing policies to achieve sustainable development. They recognised sustainable development as an overarching goal for the OECD and its Member countries, and asked the Organisation to:

- develop agreed indicators that measure progress across all three dimensions of sustainable development;

- identify how obstacles to policy reforms, in particular to the better use of market-based instruments and to the reduction of environmentally harmful subsidies, can be overcome, and deepen its analytical work on these instruments;

- analyse further the social aspects of sustainable development; and

- provide guidance for achieving improved economic, environmental and social policy coherence and integration.

The Ministers renewed their long-standing commitment to reduce trade-distorting and environmentally harmful subsidies in 2002. These subsidies were also highlighted at the World Summit on Sustainable Development held in Johannesburg in September 2002, and in the adopted Plan of Implementation.

As a first response to the Mandate the OECD organised a Workshop on Environmentally Harmful Subsidies in November 2002. This technical Workshop was an important step in the response to the high-level mandates, involving the Directorate of Food, Agriculture and Fisheries; the Environment Directorate; the Directorate for Science, Technology and Industry, the Trade Directorate; the International Energy Agency; and the European Conference of Ministers of Transport.

The objectives of the Workshop were to:

- develop a shared understanding of the methodologies used in subsidy measurement;

- identify information and analytical gaps standing in the way of progress; and

- define a way forward for the OECD work on environmentally harmful subsidies.

3

This was the first time that the OECD had addressed the overall definition of subsidies and sought to identify those that are environmentally harmful, in a cross-sectoral manner. Most analysis to date has been undertaken sector by sector, often in isolation. Although the Workshop focused on the environmental dimension, several participants emphasised the need to analyse subsidies in the wider context of sustainable development.

As the Deputy Secretary-General responsible for the OECD work on sustainable development, I have a strong commitment to advance work in this area and to contribute actively to the work itself. I also believe that subsidies are one of the areas where the OECD can and should make a contribution in the context of the Plan of Implementation of the World Summit on Sustainable Development. The OECD has been involved for a long time in measuring subsidies and developing tools for analysing them, and is internationally recognised as one of the leading organisations in the field. Also, the OECD database on environmentally related taxes provides detailed data on tax exemptions, another form of subsidy. In other words, the OECD has a clear comparative advantage in this area – and even a duty – to advance the analytical work and share our expertise on subsidies.

It is not enough just to know what the environmental impacts of subsidies are. I would now like to see the debate move to another level – to analyse the obstacles to phasing out environmentally harmful subsidies and help governments develop a strategy for their removal. Moreover, we should try to see where there are real gains to be made in phasing out subsidies that not only harm the environment, but also distort trade, penalise developing countries, and impose burdens on the poorer members in our own societies. Taking concrete steps will require political commitment and strong international co-operation. It will also require involving a wider group of stakeholders.

It is a great pleasure for me to present the proceedings of the Workshop.

Berglind Ásgeirsdóttir
Deputy Secretary General, OECD

## Acknowledgements

The OECD expresses its appreciation to all participants for contributing to the success of the Workshop. This report was prepared with the editorial assistance of Patricia Prinsen-Geerligs, Michèle Patterson, Anthony Cox and Michael Tingay.

# TABLE OF CONTENTS

# INTRODUCTION

The OECD and other institutions collect data on subsidies given to a range of sectors for different purposes, using different accounting frameworks. Yet it is possible to identify some common elements in subsidy measurement. The various concepts, definitions and measurement of subsidies were reviewed in the OECD Workshop on Environmentally Harmful Subsidies, and a start was made on determining whether subsidies are harmful for the environment, or their removal beneficial. The Workshop brought together around 100 subsidy experts from OECD countries, research institutes, international and non-governmental organisations, delegates from OECD countries and OECD Secretariat.

This publication contains four of the key papers presented at the Workshop, together with a summary of the Workshop outcomes. All of the papers that were presented at the Workshop, including background papers on measuring subsidies in different sectors and a stocktaking of available data on subsidies, are available on the OECD website (http://www1.oecd.org/agr/ehsw). A list of the papers is provided in Annex A to this report.

**David Pearce** discusses environmentally harmful subsidies in the context of sustainable development and the impact of subsidies on developing countries. He emphasises that removing such subsidies will improve overall welfare, but that there will be tradeoffs between the economic, environmental and social dimensions that need to be considered.

**Gareth Porter** reviews the state of knowledge in defining, measuring and analysing environmentally harmful subsidies across sectors, both in terms of OECD and non-OECD work, while **Ronald Steenblik** discusses the common and specific elements in measuring and classifying subsidies.

**Jan Pieters** proposes a practical approach to dealing with the challenging issue of identifying those subsidies that are environmentally harmful. Using a set of questions (or a "checklist"), the purpose is to rank different types of subsidies according to their potential environmental impact. The impact will depend on the way subsidies interact with the regulatory and resource management frameworks already in place. The checklist tests whether the subsidy operates in a way that leads to an increase in production processes with negative environmental impacts. It also assesses whether this is unavoidable, or if additional intervention could ensure clean production.

**Michel Potier** provides a summary of the Workshop and notes that, while the identification and measurement of environmentally harmful subsidies is at an early stage of development and there are many gaps, a good deal of work has been undertaken and other work is underway in the OECD. Work on developing a transparent framework for classifying subsidies, and subsidy indicators, should be pursued, building on systems of national accounts and the "checklist" approach will be tested for specific sectors.

The Workshop also suggested that the OECD could consider advancing the work over the medium term including:

- supplementing and updating existing databases on subsidies and exploring the fuller inclusion of subsidies in National Accounts;

- improving the conceptual framework for analysing the environmental impact of subsidies and testing the "checklist" in various sectors;

- strengthening co-operation between the various institutions working in this area; and

- examining the role of subsidies in the broader context of sustainable development, in order to understand the possible synergies and tradeoffs in subsidy reform.

# ENVIRONMENTALLY HARMFUL SUBSIDIES: BARRIERS TO SUSTAINABLE DEVELOPMENT

*David PEARCE*
*University College and*
*Imperial College, London*

## The issue

There is now a substantial literature that addresses the key questions relating to environmentally harmful subsidies: *a priori* reasoning on why some, and probably most, subsidies damage the environment; how subsidies are to be defined; how large they are; and the sector-by-sector effects of subsidies on the environment (Kosmo, 1987; OECD, 1996, 1997; de Moor and Calamai, 1997; OECD, 1998; Myers and Kent, 1998; Sizer, 2000; van Beers and de Moor, 2001; van Beers and van den Bergh, 2001; Porter, 2002). The literature addressing the issue of what in practice can be done to reduce subsidies — what we might call the 'political economy' of subsidies — is far smaller (Pearce and Finck von Finckenstein, 1999; van Beers and de Moor, 2001). There remains, however, a need to define subsidies carefully to determine which are environmentally damaging, to detail the criteria by which their effects can be judged beneficial or detrimental to the goal of sustainable development, and to obtain a better appreciation of just how large subsidies are.

Definitions do matter. Subsidies are not always easy to identify and there are problems of baseline comparison. For example, international aviation fuel is not taxed, but it is not explicitly subsidised in the sense of cash transfers from the public purse to the oil or aviation industry. Many would argue, however, that the absence of a tax constitutes a subsidy because zero taxation is not practised on other competing modes of transport. There are clearly problems of defining the appropriate baseline.

Determining the *effects* of subsidies also matters. Even if it can be demonstrated that a given subsidy harms the environment relative to a baseline in which the subsidy does not exist, the subsidy may serve some other social purpose. For example, some OECD countries practise differential household energy sector taxation in order to protect low income and other socially vulnerable households. The absence of a tax, or the existence of lower taxes in the household sector, can be viewed as a subsidy. While there may be disagreements about the efficiency of achieving social goals through subsidies, the fact is that there may well be a trade-off between environmental damage and the achievement of socially fair taxation. Hence, while the focus of this Workshop is quite rightly on environmentally harmful subsidies, it is not sufficient to cease the analysis once environmentally harm has been determined. The social and economic effects must also be gauged so that any trade-offs can be highlighted.

Finally, *measuring the scale* of subsidies matters. It may or may not matter too much if global subsidies are USD 1 trillion or USD 1.2 trillion, but the general size matters because of what we might call the 'demonstration effect'. Media headlines are far more likely to ensue if it is observed that global subsidies are twenty times the scale of official annual foreign aid, than if they are a few hundreds of billions of dollars. Along with scale, it is vital to know how subsidies vary between rich and poor countries and in which economic sectors they are concentrated. Table 1 repeats the estimates in van Beers and de Moor (2001).[1]

However uncertain these estimates are, the general implications are clear. Subsidies probably total over USD 1 trillion per year. Around two thirds of the subsidies occur in OECD countries. Those OECD subsidies are heavily concentrated in agriculture, mining, road transport and manufacturing. Non-OECD countries mainly subsidise energy, water, fisheries and some agriculture. Relative to GDP, subsidies are twice as large in non-OECD countries. As a percentage of world GDP, global subsidies account for a staggering 4%. Perhaps most notable of all, agricultural subsidies in OECD countries account for over 30% of all subsidies.

The environmental implications of the subsidies listed in Table 1 are potentially substantial.

## Table 1. Estimates of world subsidies 1994-98
(USD billion)

|  | OECD | Non-OECD | World | OECD as % of world |
|---|---|---|---|---|
| *Natural resource sectors* | | | | |
| Agriculture | 335 | 65 | 400 | 84 |
| Water | 15 | 45 | 60 | 25 |
| Forestry | 5 | 30 | 35 | 4 |
| Fisheries | 10 | 10 | 20 | 50 |
| Mining | 25 | 5 | 30 | 83 |
| *Energy and industry sectors* | | | | |
| Energy | 80 | 160 | 240 | 33 |
| Road transport | 200 | 25 | 225 | 89 |
| Manufacturing | 55 | negligible | 55 | 100 |
| **Total** | **725** | **340** | **1 065** | **68** |
| Total as% GDP | 3.4 | 6.3 | 4.0 | |

*Notes*
- As the basis for Table 1 is fragmented, it involves expected differences.
- Subsidy estimates in Van Beers and de Moor (2001) for OECD countries are in general based on OECD sources. However, many of these OECD sources only cover a part of OECD. Other sources on OECD countries used obtain broader coverage; these have been checked and assessed on their validity and subsidy methodology.
- Agriculture: same source for OECD, no differences except for year.
- Transport:
  ➢ difference in coverage. OECD (2002) covers European countries, while Van Beers and de Moor (2001) includes US and Japan. In particular, the US accounts for a large part in road transport subsidies
  ➢ difference in definition: OECD (2002) mentions social costs, suggesting that it includes costs of congestion; Van Beers and de Moor (2001) do not.
  ➢ difference in sector: OECD (2002) includes rail; Van Beers and de Moor (2001) do not.
- Energy:
  ➢ difference in coverage: OECD (2002) is likely to include only coal subsidies in a few European countries. Van Beers and de Moor (2001) include all energy support in more and major OECD countries, for example US and Canada.
  ➢ difference in definition: OECD (2002) mentions subsidies to energy production which suggests a narrower definition than Van Beers and de Moor (2001).
  ➢ difference in year: OECD (2002) covers 1999 while Van Beers and de Moor (2001) do not.
- Manufacturing/shipbuilding/steel:
  ➢ difference in coverage: OECD (2002) only includes EU. Van Beers and de Moor (2001) have a much wider OECD coverage (based on OECD survey, 1993 and 1998).
- Fisheries:
  ➢ OECD (2002) seems to include financial transfers while Van Beers and de Moor (2001) also include tax expenditures and the inadequacy to cover the full economic rent from fish resources.
- Water: no adequate information to assess differences.
- Forestry: no adequate information to assess differences.
- Mining: based on a case study for the US and on macro indicators.

*Source* : van Beers et de Moor (2001).

11

First, the pervasiveness of subsidies means that economic activity in the relevant sectors will be larger than is justified. In so far as environmental damage is a linear function of the *scale* of economic activity, subsidies produce higher levels of environmental damage than can be considered 'optimal'.

Second, the *nature* of the subsidies matters. It is not appropriate in an overview paper to explore definitional classifications in any detail, but most writers make a distinction between *(a)* market price support, *(b)* cost-reducing payments, and *(c)* payments for explicit environmental purposes. Price guarantees, such that prices for output produced exceed world prices, encourage over-production and hence environmental damage. The nature of the price guarantee matters. Subsidies that vary with the scale of *production* are likely to be more environmentally harmful than subsidies that contain some element of *decoupling*, *e.g.* direct payments unrelated to output. Environmentally harmful effects in the agricultural sector, for example, arise because maximum subsidy receipts are secured by maximising production which in turn means (a) switching to intensive production techniques, and (b) extensifying production on to marginal lands and environmentally valuable areas such as woodlands, ponds, hedgerows, etc. Such direct payments may be linked to various conditions, as with the 1992 McSharry reforms under the Common Agricultural Policy in the European Union. Cost-reducing subsidies will have similar effects to price guarantees. Finally, subsidies may take the form of direct payments for environmental services. How far such payments deserve the title 'subsidy' is open to debate. Paying a producer to do something he or she would not otherwise have done is an effective subsidy, but paying for a voluntarily provided external environmental benefit might be better thought of as an example of a 'beneficiary pays' principle.

Even if it could be argued that subsidies serve some social or economic development goals, a rational look at the costs and benefits of subsidies would at least raise the right questions. Are the trade-offs that are virtually certain to arise with subsidies such that overall net benefits are being secured? If they serve some distributional goal, are those distributional benefits worth the economic and environmental costs? The underlying suspicion must be that the vast majority of these subsidies not only fail a conventional cost-benefit test, but that most of them fail to support the incomes of low income or vulnerable groups in society. In the context of water subsidies in the developing world, for example, where the 'protect the poor' argument is frequently voiced, Briscoe (1997) points to the 'hydraulic law of subsidies'. Since politicians interfere in water pricing, the effect is rarely one of protecting the poor but of actually placing them at further disadvantage. Below-cost tariffs result in losses for public water utilities that cannot then invest in proper services. The scramble for the supplies that are provided results in the better off securing supplies, and the poor often having to resort to high cost vendors of water. The subsidies themselves actually produce the failure to protect the poor, however their objective is first formulated.

The geographical 'footprint' of the subsidies matters too. While many subsidies appear to be locally focused, the geographical extent of the effects of the subsidies listed in Table 1 is often global. The World Bank (2002) estimates that rich country industrial and agricultural protection policies impose costs of USD 100 billion annually on poor countries. What is not always recognised is that this formidable income loss — roughly twice the level of official foreign aid to developing countries — itself has environmental consequences. Poverty itself is directly linked to environmental degradation as economic agents seek to utilise the 'free' resources of nature to supplement meagre incomes. Local people will also have to switch to more marginal environmental resources if they cannot compete with subsidised exploitation of more plentiful resources by protected rich countries, a feature that is especially important in fisheries.

This brief overview suggests the following interim conclusions:

1.  There is a *prima facie* case for supposing that subsidies which encourage more production will be environmentally harmful. Subsidies that try to decouple payment from output levels are less environmentally harmful, but still have the effect of keeping production in existence when the optimal solution may be for it to cease altogether.

2.  Subsidies that seek to insulate domestic production from international competition are likely to have further environmentally harmful effects in the countries facing trade barriers.

3.  Payments for environmental services can be seen as subsidies or as justified internalisation of external benefits, the view taken depending on the assumed allocation of property rights between producers and environmental beneficiaries.

## Sustainable development

Subsidies are linked to sustainable development in a number of ways. In order to provide a framework for analysing these effects we first sketch the theory of sustainable development (for a slightly more extended treatment, see Pearce, 1999).

'Sustainable' simply means that the goal in question lasts through time. The choice of time horizon is problematic. Some of the sustainable development literature appears to think of time horizons as infinite. This almost certainly confuses sustainability with survivability, maximising the time period over which humans occupy the earth. That might easily be maximised if everyone opted for a subsistence standard of living. Few would vote for such a future. Hence sustainable development must refer to sustaining at least current levels of human wellbeing over some reasonable but finite time horizon. 'Development' is a value-word: its meaning will vary with what those defining it consider being the constituents of a 'developed' nation. Development occurs if at least average human wellbeing rises over time, and, ideally, the wellbeing of the poorest rises much faster than that of the richest. Precisely what the constituents of wellbeing are may not matter very much if the *conditions* for achieving a sustained development are common to all goals.

What determines the ability of a given set of humans to improve their wellbeing? The ability to create productive capacity is determined by the quantity and quality of capital assets available at the time. It is important to understand what these capital assets are, and this issue has been explored extensively in the sustainable development literature. Capital stocks can be decomposed into *man-made capital*, $K_M$; *natural capital* ($K_N$), human capital ($K_h$) and social capital ($IC_s$). Natural capital refers to traditionally defined natural resources, such as oil or gas, forests and to the stocks of assimilative capacities in the environment. Rivers, oceans and the atmosphere act as receiving media for wastes generated by economic activity and they can therefore be thought of as a capital stock yielding a flow of assimilation services. In general, what ecologists call ecological services are all economic services yielded by natural capital. Human capital refers to the stock of knowledge and skills embodied in humans. Social capital is variously defined but has something to do with the set of interpersonal relationships and institutional relationships that hold society together. A society with a greater degree of trust between individuals is a society with more social capital. A society that is corrupt and lawless has less social capital.

The productivity of all these forms of capital — their ability to generate human wellbeing — can be enhanced through *technological change*. But the ability of capital stocks to generate increases in per capita wellbeing is almost certainly decreased by population growth. As a general rule, and one that emerges from the growth economics literature of the 1970s, technological change must exceed population growth if sustainable development is to be assured. The more general rule for sustainable development is that the *technology-weighted index of per capita capital stocks must rise through time.*

This is the 'constant capital rule' for sustainable development (Atkinson *et al.*, 1997).

The rule for sustainable development can now be fairly easily stated.

$$\dot{k} = \frac{d}{dt}\left(\frac{K}{N}\right) = \frac{K}{N}\left(\frac{\dot{K}}{K} - \frac{\dot{N}}{N}\right) = \frac{K}{N}\left(\frac{\dot{K}}{K} - n\right) > 0 \qquad [1]^2$$

where $\dot{k}$ is the rate of change in per capita stocks of overall capital, K is the stock of all capital assets - also known as 'wealth' (*i.e.* $K_M + K_H + K_N$, and leaving aside $K_S$ due to measurement difficulties), N is population and $n$ is the rate of change of population. Note that K is wealth and $\dot{K}$ is the rate of change in wealth, which is formally equivalent to *genuine savings*. Genuine savings is simply gross savings (or investment) less the depreciation on all forms of capital. Intuition tells us that savings need to exceed capital depreciation for they're to be net additions to the capital stock. Hence we can always write:

$$\dot{K} = S_g \qquad [2]$$

The requirement that changes be in per capita terms makes the 'wealth per capita rule' different to the 'genuine savings' rule for sustainability previously advocated for measuring sustainability (Pearce, 2000).

Research at the World Bank has developed sets of estimates for wealth per capita (Hamilton and Clemens, 1999; Hamilton, 2000). Take the example of the United States. The computation for the year 1997 produces the following results:

K/N =       wealth per capita       =   USD 535 000

$S_g$/N= $\dot{K}/N$  =  genuine savings per capita =   USD 3 900

n =    population growth rate   =   0.008

Putting these values into equation [1] yields the change in wealth per capita as -USD 380, a *negative* change in wealth. Despite having a positive genuine savings per capita, the overall change in wealth per capita is negative. Changing the assumptions has a marked effect on this result. If genuine savings per capita is measured to be USD 4 100 instead of USD 3 900 the effect is to

may not end until the level of phosphorus load is reduced by 40% (Brouwer, 2002).

Studies that attempt to quantify the environmental impacts of a multilateral trade liberalisation agreement on particular agricultural sub-sectors raise additional issues beyond those associated with a single country subsidy reform case study or a cross-sectional study based on subsidy reform at the national level. Trade liberalisation is not the primary factor in determining trade patterns, so assessments of trade liberalisation agreements, whether *ex ante* or *ex post*, must distinguish the effect of trade liberalisation on changes in trade from other powerful factors, such as relative price changes, changes in income and consumer tastes, and exchange rates. This can be done by examining historical trends in tariffs and trade and by partial-equilibrium models which allow the analyst to isolate the effect of trade liberalisation from other effects in a particular sector. Once that analytical problem has been solved, the increased exports and imports must be translated into impacts on production in the products selected for study in order to estimate the changes in the level of stresses on the environment. A joint study by the OECD's Directorate for Food, Agriculture and Fisheries and the Directorate for the Environment (OECD, 2000) projects trade liberalisation-induced changes in the production of wheat, coarse grains and rice in eight OECD countries, based on its Aglink model, and shows how those changes are related to rate of pesticide use per hectare and in nitrogen surplus per hectare for the same countries. It shows that the increased production from trade liberalisation will take place in those OECD countries with lower indices of agri-chemical pollution, while the EU and Japan, who have considerably higher indices of agri-chemical pollution, are projected to lose production under trade liberalisation. However, it does not try to quantify the changes in pesticide and nitrogen use likely to result from trade liberalisation.

A key issue in the *ex post* analysis of the environmental impacts of trade liberalisation agreements on specific agricultural sub-sectors is whether the additional exports that may be attributable to such an agreement were on a scale large enough to alter the level of production in a way that bears on the environment. The extremely limited character of the agricultural trade liberalisation achieved at the global level thus far is indicated by the fact that the value of agricultural commodity exports since the Uruguay Round Agricultural Agreement (URAA) have sharply declined, contrary to the general view that trade liberalisation should raise global commodity prices (Convention of Biodiversity, 2002).

A study of the impacts of the North American Free Trade Agreement and the Uruguay Round Agreement on Agriculture on North American beef, corn and tomato sub-sectors (Porter, 2003) suggests that the liberalisation in most agricultural sectors in those two agreements was too small to make a difference in production patterns. He observes that the production effects of increased exports in each of the three sectors were reduced to negligible proportions by the relatively small size of the incremental exports in relation to domestic production, major increases in yield that have halted growth in area planted, and by the relative unresponsiveness of the corn and beef sub-sectors to price signals. At least in most sub-sectors and in most countries, therefore, the modest liberalisation of agricultural trade achieved thus far is unlikely to have had any significant impacts on the environment, either positive or negative.

Economists try to capture not only the direct effects on trade patterns and production in specific agricultural sub-sectors, but also the effects on all sectors of the economy and to measure second and third-level impacts. Second-level impacts are those resulting from interactions between and among markets and production, not only in agriculture but in other sectors of the economies. The third-level impacts are the economic equilibrium, or economic adjustment effects, resulting from first- and second-level impacts, such as changes in consumer spending and employment patterns. For these purposes, analysts use computable general equilibrium (CGE) models. The CGE model is run twice, first to simulate conditions in a "base year" without the trade liberalisation agreement, and then a second time with all other macroeconomic conditions in that same year remaining the same but simulating the trade liberalisation agreement in effect (Gallagher et al., 2002).

CGE models predict the effect of a given set of trade policy changes on the basis of a large and complex set of assumptions about relationships, especially price elasticities of supply and demand in specific industries, or in the case of agriculture, specific crops. These assumptions are in turn derived from economic theory, but the model must make a number of arbitrary assumptions about these relationships, which are highly uncertain. These models can only provide snapshots of relatively short-tem effects, moreover, rather than predict longer-term changes. A number of ex ante analyses of the trade effects of NAFTA were grossly inaccurate in their predictions of trade patterns between the United States and Mexico (Gallagher et al., 2002). Such failures strongly suggest that the likelihood of being able to predict the kinds of macroeconomic shocks that largely determine actual levels of trade are quite small.

The USDA's Economic Research Service (ERS) has used a computable general equilibrium (CGE) model to estimate changes in production of various agricultural commodities by country from different agricultural support scenarios in a multilateral trade agreement (Young et al., 2001), but has not yet attempted to derive any estimates of changes in pesticide or fertiliser use from those data. However, the ERS has estimated changes in agricultural pollution in the United States that would result from the creation of a Free Trade Area of the Americas (FTAA) (FTAA Interagency Environment Program, 2000). The study uses a mathematical programming model of the US agricultural sector (the US Department of Agriculture's USMP model), combined with a geographic information system, to simulate changes in use of land and water resources from changes in trade flows. The model estimates changes in eight environmental indicators, including soil loss from water erosion, nitrogen and phosphorus losses to atmosphere and water, carbon fluxes and greenhouse gases.[3] Some analyses are also being conducted by members of the research advisory boards to the network of GTAP users. Fertiliser subsidies can induce a considerable increase in fertiliser demand by distorting the relative prices of agrochemicals and organic sources of nutrients, such as animal manure and sewage and thus discouraging the use of the latter (Runge-Metzger, 1996). Ending fertiliser subsidies has had an immediate and dramatic effect on fertiliser use. When New Zealand ended its subsidies to fertilisers in 1986 after two years' notice, fertiliser sales fell by nearly half. Fertiliser consumption in Czechoslovakia, Hungary and Poland fell by even greater percentages after fertiliser subsidies were ended there in 1990. Subsidy reform does not account for all of the reduction in any of these cases, but it is by far the most important reason (OECD, 1998b).

A demand curve for fertiliser can be constructed on the basis of historical data for both subsidised and unsubsidised prices, as has been done for Ghana for the 1980-89 period. On the basis of that demand curve, the decrease in fertiliser use from subsidy removal or reduction can be predicted at least in the short run. In most countries, the slope of the demand curve for chemical fertiliser depends on the fertiliser-product price ratios in the particular economy. An econometric study of 11 Asian countries shows that the demand for chemical fertiliser was relatively sensitive to the price ratio of rice to fertiliser — an elasticity between 0.4 and 0.7 in the short run, and even higher in the long run (Barker *et al.*, 1985). Thus, in countries in which new varieties and irrigation are sharply increasing, demand for fertiliser is relatively inelastic (Runge-Metzger, 1996; Hedley and Tabor, 1989). Subsidy elimination usually means that prices will increase by very large percentages, however, so even a very inelastic response translates into a very significant reduction in demand. In Indonesia, when fertiliser subsidies were removed in 1999, the price of urea increased by 150%, while paddy prices increased by only 50%. Although the elasticity of demand in response to this change was only -0.2, the result was a 30% decline in consumption compared with the previous year (Soedjais, 1999).

Longer-term responses to the change in relative prices, however, depend on the further evolution of the fertiliser-product price ratio. Increased world prices for crops can increase the use of fertiliser even after subsidy removal. After the New Zealand fertiliser sales fell sharply in response to subsidy removal, for example, they began to rise rapidly again in the early 1990s in response world market prices and by 1994 were back up to the 1983 level (OECD, 1998b). In most Sub-Saharan Africa the reduction or elimination of fertiliser subsidies in the 1980s, along with currency devaluations in connection with structural adjustment programmes, have made fertiliser much more expensive. Demand for fertiliser has varied from country to country, depending on how devaluations have affected prices for the major crops grown in the country. Export crops such as cotton and tobacco are heavily fertilised, whereas crops that are not traded internationally are fertilised much less. Thus Benin has increased fertiliser use ten-fold since the early 1980s, whereas Malawi has increased its fertiliser use by only 30% (IFPRI, 2001).

Sub-Saharan African countries present a special case in which the environmental impacts of agricultural subsidies may be positive rather than negative. In these countries, soils have suffered major losses in nitrogen and phosphorous nutrients in recent decades, and rates of fertiliser use are still only a small fraction of the global average. Fertiliser subsidies appear to be justifiable for these countries in order to reverse net nutrient depletion, reduce soil erosion and increase yields (Aune and Oygard, 1999; Warford, Munasinghe and Cruz, 1997).

Translating changes in fertilizer or pesticide use per hectare into changes in pollution levels is more complex. Cross-country and time series data for fertiliser use and agricultural land under cultivation are available from the FAO. The OECD has also compiled detailed estimates for pesticide use and nitrogen balances (the difference between input of application of nutrients entering the soil and the output or withdrawal of nutrients from the soil) for 22 OECD countries. Although total nitrogen balances at national levels are often used as a proxy indicator for nitrate pollution from chemical fertilisers and manure there are important differences between the two (Rørstad, 1999). The degree of nitrate pollution from a given nitrogen balance will depend on various characteristics of soil, climate and topography.

Aggregate national data on pesticide use is a less satisfactory environmental indicator than data on fertiliser use, because the thousands of pesticides in use have widely varying degrees of potency and toxicity. Nevertheless, Denmark's Ministry of Environment and Energy (1998) has managed to construct an "Index of Load" taking into account the toxicity and relative importance of various pesticides in total pesticide consumption to show trends in the environmental load of agricultural pesticides from a reference period (1981-85) to 1996. However, this index would not be applicable to agricultural systems in which the profile of pesticide use is substantially different.

### Data gaps and research needs

In addition to the continuing collection and reporting of data on agricultural support by OECD countries, the WTO Trade Policy Reviews are now the primary source of data on various types of agricultural support. A careful review, collation and analysis of support data in such reviews in recent years for countries not covered by the OECD system would appear to be a good basis for attempting to establish a broader disaggregated agricultural support database. Very little *ex post* analysis has been done to estimate the environmental impacts of a specific agricultural trade liberalisation agreement on specific crop or livestock sub-sectors. It would not require a major research effort to cover all the major sub-sectors for both NAFTA and the URAA. Such empirical research would provide a more solid basis for analyses of a possible future trade liberalisation agreement than now exists.

Systematic research and analysis on causal linkages between subsidies and environmental issues in agriculture has been focused almost entirely on OECD countries themselves. No studies have addressed the question of how subsidies in OECD countries affect the environment in specific agricultural sub-sectors of developing countries or how trade liberalization in such highly protected sectors as sugar or cotton would affect the environment in developing countries producing those crops. Such studies would need to consider the potential trade-offs between additional environmental stresses from increased production in developing countries and reduced production in highly subsidized OECD countries.

## Irrigation water

### Distinguishing characteristics of the sector

- Although irrigation subsidies could be considered as a subset of agricultural subsidies, its significance also transcends the agricultural sector. Irrigation accounts for 75% to 90% of total water use in developing countries (World Bank, 2001), and for more than one-third of water use in many OECD countries, so irrigation water subsidies can have major affects on water resource allocation.

- Infrastructure used in the provision of water for irrigation is often shared with other users of water, including hydro-electric works.

- Water is a resource that often cannot be used in agriculture without capital investments that are normally too large for individual communities to bear. By financing those investments, the government effectively confers a significant resource rent on a relatively limited group of beneficiaries.

- Incomplete property rights are pervasive, encouraging over-exploitation of ground-water resources on the part of irrigators who draw from the same aquifers (Tsur, 2000; Ringler et al., 2000).

- Water supplies have "lumpy" cost curves with discontinuities, and the supplier from a river-fed reservoir has high fixed costs and low variable costs as in a natural monopoly (Hall, 2000).

- With few exceptions, no internalisation of environmental externalities or of the resource depletion costs associated with irrigation is taking place through the pricing of irrigation water. The state's involvement in making irrigation possible, raises the issue of whether the absence of internalization of these costs confers additional benefits to irrigators and should thus be considered as a subsidy.

### Defining and measuring irrigation water subsidies

Practitioners have defined a subsidy to the supply of irrigation water in two ways. The first, which is sometimes called the "cost-recovery" approach, defines it as public expenditures that benefit irrigators, net of the revenues from water charges paid by irrigators.[4] When small-scale irrigation works are involved, the measurement of these expenditures is generally straightforward (though data are often hard to obtain). Budgetary expenditures for each project are small, and therefore in the aggregate are less "lumpy" than for larger projects. Calculating gross costs attributable to irrigators for large (often publicly owned), surface-water-fed irrigation works is much more difficult, for several reasons. First, construction costs are often spread out over many years before the water is actually delivered to irrigators. Second, often the infrastructure and reservoirs are common to, for example, irrigation and other water uses, or irrigation and hydro-electric works. Third, governments usually levy some charge aimed at recovering some of these costs, but typically the pricing formulae employed attribute large portions of the project's costs to "public" uses (*e.g.* recreational boating) or to other private users (*e.g.* through cross-subsidies from electricity consumers), and use a rate of interest in the amortisation calculation that is below what a private entity would use. Calculating this degree of under-pricing on a project-by-project basis for a large country with multiple irrigation works of widely varying vintage would be an enormous task.

In addition to paying less than the full attributable costs of government-provided capital investments, irrigators are also supported through costs incurred by governments to cover the operation and maintenance of irrigation systems. These costs include the costs of personnel, materials and electricity for pumping, but also — in the view of some researchers — any foregone revenues that could have been earned by public utilities by running diverted water through hydro-electric turbines. Harden (1996) estimates, for example, that the opportunity cost to the federally owned Bonneville Power Administration (BPA) of diverting water from behind its Grand Coulee Dam hydro-electric plant to farms within the Columbia Basin Irrigation Project amounts to between USD 150 and USD 300 million a year. That is in addition to the opportunity cost to BPA of pumping the water up several hundred metres and charging irrigators only 1/28 of the retail price for the service. Special low electricity prices are also offered in some countries for private irrigators, mainly for pumping ground-water.

When it addresses cost recovery, the literature on irrigation water pricing generally does not include environmental and resources costs that are not otherwise internalized within the scope of costs that should be recovered. However, the European Commission has called, in a policy paper on water pricing policies, for the inclusion of marginal environmental and resources costs in the costs that should be recovered in the pricing of agricultural irrigation water, as well as water for household and industrial use (Commission of the European Communities, 2000). This implied that the Commission regards environmental and resource costs that are not recovered by the authority providing water as a subsidy to the user.

The cost-recovery definition of subsidies can be expressed either as an absolute value of net public spending or as the percentage of annual total expenditures not covered by revenues from water charges.

The second method of defining a subsidy to irrigators is based on the actual value of the water to the irrigator rather than the amount of public expenditure. According to this definition, an irrigation subsidy would be the difference between the water's net economic benefit to the irrigator per unit and the charged price per unit. Economists consider this difference to be a "rent" conferred on irrigators by the water authority and have used this definition of irrigation water subsidy to understand the degree of distortion introduced into the agricultural economy by under-pricing the resource (Diao and Roe, 2000). The price that is based on the resource rent obtained from the water by the irrigator is also called the "shadow price" (Tiwari and Dinar, 2001; Lofgren, 1995). This value of the water to the irrigator is the marginal value product (MVP) of the water,[5] which is based on the incremental yield, or marginal physical product (MPP), of the water (Tiwari, 1998; Tiwari and Dinar, 2001). Ordinarily, the MPP is calculated based on a generic crop-water production function or on farm-level budget data. If both dry land and irrigated crops are produced within a homogeneous growing region, however, the MVP can be estimated by comparing the average commercial value of yield from irrigated lands in the district with the average yield on non-irrigated lands (Gardner, 1983). When water rights are traded, as in the western states of the US, the market value of the land incorporates the MVP of the water (Cummings and Nercissiantz, 1992). Land-value differentials thus provide yet another method of measuring the rent implicit in access to irrigation water and thus calculating the subsidy (Cummings and Nercissiantz, 1992).

### *Country-by-country irrigation water subsidy data available*

No intergovernmental organisation or non-governmental organisation is now engaged in ongoing collection and reporting of data on irrigation water subsidies. However, some data have been collected using one or the other of the two definitions of irrigation water subsidy, by OECD, the World Bank and some independent researchers. The OECD has compiled rough estimates on the ratio of operations and maintenance costs as well as capital costs for 15 OECD countries. The percentage of operations and maintenance costs recovered by irrigation water prices (median or as ranges) have been published by the OECD Environment Directorate (1999) for various years from 1995 to 1998. These data are disaggregated by agricultural region for nine of the countries covered, and national averages are indicated for seven countries, with both regional rates and national averages given for two countries. These data suggest that most OECD countries were recovering operations and maintenance costs on irrigation systems, and that at least two (The Netherlands and New Zealand) were recovering some fraction of capital costs as well). They show that Greece, Italy, Mexico and Turkey were recovering only about 60 to 75% of operations and maintenance costs.

Eurostat, the statistical office of the European Communities, has adopted plans for documenting current cost and price levels for irrigation water in selected EU members, beginning with pilot studies in Luxembourg and Spain (Commission of the European Communities, 2000). A search of the Eurostat website did not turn up any additional documentation on these plans.

The World Bank has studied irrigation water pricing experiences in a number of countries, but has not done any systematic data collection on government spending on irrigation systems or on revenues from irrigation water charges. In a study of irrigation water pricing focused on five countries, Tsur *et al.* (2002) provided recent data on the proportion of costs recovered by irrigation water prices in South Africa, Mexico and Morocco, but provides no precise data on the ratio for Turkey and is unclear on whether or not "supply costs" include capital costs in China. The case studies do not provide data on actual budgetary expenditures on irrigation water systems in the three countries.

In its calculation of support to agricultural producers, OECD includes some estimates of government expenditure on on-farm irrigation works, operation and maintenance costs and, for a few countries, capital projects. However, the data are highly aggregate and not comprehensive.

Several studies have produced detailed data on estimated subsidies for several countries based on the resource rent definition. Saleth (1997) has compiled data on for 13 states of India for 1989-90 showing irrigation water prices as a percentage of net economic benefit, measured by the difference between incremental yield from irrigated lands and from non-irrigated lands. Diao and Roe (2000) report on data they have collected in Morocco comparing water's contribution to the gross value of irrigated agricultural outputs and the relationship between water charges and the value of those outputs in nine regional development authorities responsible for water resources management.

Bowen and Young (1985) have used a linear programming model to derive estimates of financial and economic net benefits to irrigation water supply for a case study area in the northern Nile delta of Egypt. Hussein and Young (1985) have estimated the net economic benefits of irrigation water for irrigators in Pakistan. Perry (2001) estimates the typical subsidy to irrigation water in Iran to be 90% of the full economic value of the water. In 1989, the national water authority in Mexico estimated the net economic value of water in northwest Mexico, and similar estimates of MVP were made in northern irrigation districts in the United States. In the early 1990s irrigation water subsidies in those districts were estimated at about 60% of the value of the water (Cummings and Nercissiantz, 1992).

*Methodologies for estimating potential environmental impacts of subsidy removal*

Under-pricing of water through irrigation subsidies has two kinds of impacts on the environment, both related to the excessive withdrawal of water:

the first is that, in regions in which irrigation would not have been profitable on some or all of the land without a subsidy, it artificially increases the area of land that is irrigated. The second is that it results in inefficient management of water on irrigated land (Rosegrant, 1997). When water charges are based on irrigated area, rather than on the amount of water used, they undervalue water resources. A study of various irrigation projects in Brazil reveals that the single most important cause of the water loss is excessive length of irrigation time (Ringler et al., 2000), which is directly related to the lack of incentive to use the resource efficiently. Water tariffs based on area are by far the most prevalent worldwide. In a survey of farmers utilising 12.2 million hectares of irrigated land worldwide, Bos and Walters (1990) found that more than 60% paid charges on a per-unit-area basis, and that only about 25% paid water charges based on the volume of water used.

Prices based on volume used rather than on number of hectares irrigated can provide at least some incentive for irrigators to reduce water use by reducing the length of time that crops are irrigated, if the system can be enforced. According to a report by the US Embassy in Beijing, previous experiences in Northern China showed that simply shifting from pricing based on land area to pricing based on volume reduced total irrigation water withdrawals by 20% (Anon., 1997). But prices set at or near the MVP of the water should give irrigators the maximum incentive to reduce water consumption by adopting water-saving technologies, shifting to less water-intensive crops and reducing the amount of irrigated land (Lallana et al., 2001; Varela-Ortega et al., 1998). When the charges do approximate the MVP, the impact on water use is dramatic: Israel set the water price close to the MVP and achieved a 50% reduction in water use (Tiwari and Dinar, 2001).

All of these changes reduce the amount of water withdrawn, thus increasing instream flows of water and the amount of water remaining for other purposes. Using shadow prices to set water charges therefore reduces all the environmental impacts of the irrigation. However, it cannot actually reduce the salinization that has already occurred. Thus in places like the Aral Sea Region, where salinization has become acute, a tax on salt discharge is a much more effective means of reducing the further salinization of water resources than increasing the irrigation water tariff (Cai et al., 2001a).

One study using a mathematical programming model (MPM) that specifies crop water requirements and water application costs, and calculating farm surpluses over a 20-year time horizon estimates the charges or combination of charges and bonuses that would be required to achieve 10%, 25% and 50% reductions in irrigation water consumption for six water districts in three Spanish regions (Varela-Ortega et al., 1998). The study calculates the results of four pricing scenarios: a volumetric charge, a bloc-rate charge, a volumetric charge with a bonus for volume of water saved, and a block-rate charge with both penalty and bonus charges for quantities above and below 80% of the water allotment right. The simulation showed that the volumetric charge with bonus scheme cost the irrigators only half as much on average to achieve the 10% and 25% reduction goals and 34% less to achieve the 50% reduction. That suggests that combining optimum water charges with bonuses for water savings may be an effective way to influence irrigator practices. It also found that the technical endowments of the water districts (*i.e.* whether the district already has more efficient irrigation technologies) decisively influences both the degree of response to a given price increase as well as the impact of a given price increase on incomes.

The resource rent definition of subsidy provides an alternative approach to calculating the environmental consequences of subsidy removal. The price that approximates the MVP of the water represents the threshold price at which demand for irrigation water becomes elastic. Below that threshold, price increases will affect profitability but will not cause the irrigator to use any less water. However, prices at or near that threshold are expected to reduce or eliminate excessive water use (Tiwari and Dinar, 2001). The fact that prices for irrigation water have been far below the economic value of the water explains why researchers have consistently found irrigation water to be very price inelastic at lower prices but very price elastic above a certain threshold price (Lallana *et al.*, 2001; Varela-Ortega *et al.*, 1998). For example, OECD (1999c) reports data from institutional price simulations showing price elasticity of irrigation water demand in the Andalusian region of Spain at only -0.06 at the low end of the price ranges but -1.00 at "medium" prices ranges, and a simulation using a dynamic mathematical programming model showed an elasticity of -0.12 for the low ranges and -0.48 for "medium" price ranges for the same region.

Such calculations assume, of course, that volumetric pricing is both technically and economically feasible and politically possible. Many irrigation specialists argue that establishing volumetric pricing and raising water tariffs to the level necessary to bring about substantial savings in irrigation water would be too costly to make the "first-best" solution (even for full-cost recovery) a practical alternative, because of the large transaction costs necessary to establish volumetric pricing (Sampath, 1992; Tsur and Dinar, 1997; Spencer and Subramanian, 1997; Tsur, 2000; Perry, 2001; Tsur *et al.*, 2002). Its technical feasibility has also been questioned, given the existing infrastructure, management and regulatory frameworks (Perry, 2001).

*Data gaps and additional research needed*

Data on environmental indicators related to irrigation water remain very sparse. Data are needed on such indicators as rate of flow in watercourses, level of nitrates in water, soil toxicities and micro-nutrient deficiencies, level of groundwater table, and loss of productivity of land due to salinization at the water basin level both before and after the changes in subsidy levels. It is not clear from the available literature whether water authorities environmental agencies in the target countries or regions are already collecting any or all of these data.

## Fisheries

*Distinguishing characteristics of the sector*

- In most fisheries, property rights are absent, and the fish remain a "common-pool" resource, even though a management regime may be imposing controls on both access and effort. Thus fishers generally have a stronger incentive to maximise production in the shortest possible time than would be the case with tradable quota rights. Systems of controls on catch and effort can mitigate but not eliminate this economic incentive problem.

- Fishing fleet capacity, defined as the maximum amount of fish that a fleet fishing in a particular fishery can catch in the absence of constraints on the availability of variable factors of production (Vestergaard, Squires and Kirkley, 1999; Lindebo, 1999), is an intermediate link between subsidies and environmental impacts. In theory, subsidies can affect fisheries resources by increasing fishing effort or fleet capacity, by reducing capacity or by slowing the reduction of that capacity.

- The non-malleability of fishing fleet capital is central to the over-capacity problem. Contrary to the assumption that capital in the fisheries sector can always move to a more profitable sector if overcapitalisation makes the fisheries sector unprofitable, fixed investment costs in the fisheries sector are so high relative to operating costs that vessel owners are very slow to respond to price signals (Munro, 1999; Munro and Sumaila, 2001). This characteristic of fisheries makes for a pronounced lack of symmetry in the environmental effects of introducing new subsidies to the sector, on the one hand, and removing subsidies to the sector, on the other. However, in all cases, the actual environmental effects of subsidies (including those intended to retire capacity) depend critically on the

51

effectiveness of the accompanying management system in limiting the catch.

- Uncollected resource rents are generally not a significant subsidy issue once a fishery is over-capitalized because resource rents tend to be dissipated (Clark and Munro, 1994). When a distant-water fleet gains privileged access to a coastal state's resources under a bilateral access agreement, while paying only a very small access fee, however, uncollected resource rents may represent a substantial subsidy to the producer (Porter, 1997).

- In most fisheries, the environmental costs of fishing are not internalized in the costs of fishing licenses (Milazzo, 1998).

## *Defining and measuring fisheries subsidies*

Government financial transfers to the fisheries sector have a range of objectives and employ different methods to achieve them. The main method for estimating total subsidies to the fisheries sector is to aggregate all the financial transfers that alter the incentive structure of the fisheries sector by increasing revenues or reducing costs. Studies that have attempted to aggregate these data for OECD and APEC member states (OECD, 2000a; PricewaterhouseCoopers, 2000) have included the following types of transfers:

- direct payments to producer and processors from government budgets;

- transfers, including tax expenditures not specifically recorded in budget documents, that reduce the costs of fixed capital or of variable inputs;

- budgetary transfers for infrastructure or services that benefit the fishing industry or that are necessary to ensure that fishing is done sustainably;

- market price supports through trade measures;

- indirect financial transfers by distant water fishing countries to their own distant water fleets through payments to foreign governments for some part of the cost of access to their fishing grounds, which are usually treated as a subsidy to the cost of an input (WTO Committee on Trade and Environment, 2000; OECD, 2000a; Sharp, 2001); and

- general services.

Establishing an index of government support to the fishing industry for each country could be done by summing the annual values of all budgetary programs that benefit the fishing industry, adding an estimate of the annual value of price support to the industry and dividing by landed value of the fish catch for that year. Such a PSE-like index would not measure trade distortion but would be useful for maximising the transparency of support programs by allowing the relative support for the sector in each country to be compared with that of other countries. A complete accounting of subsidies in all OECD countries would require that price support be included. A few countries (Norway as well as Sweden and Finland before joining the European Community) have used price support measures to supplement other forms of support for fishing industries, and the EU has maintained a market price intervention program to protect fishers against low prices (OECD, 1993; OECD, 2000a). It appears, however, that price support has been sharply reduced in recent years in Norway (Milazzo, 1999; Flaaten and Wallis, 1999; OECD, 2000a). The inclusion of management services in calculation of the index for OECD countries as a whole in 1997 (without taking price support programs into account) increases the ratio of government financial transfers to the landed value of production from 4% to 17% (OECD, 2000a).[6]

### *Country-by-country fisheries subsidy data available*

In 2000 the OECD published the most complete set of estimates of government financial transfers to marine capture fisheries. The study covers direct payments, cost-reducing transfers and general services, but not price-support, for all OECD countries for 1996 and 1997. It shows the total estimates as well as figures for seven types of support programs for each country. The data also include estimates of total support as a proportion of total landed value, but without taking into account price support. This allows comparison of countries in regard to the relative weight of subsidies. The omission of price support from the estimates means that they underestimate both total and relative support, at least for some countries. However, the OECD Committee on Fisheries is expected to undertake a separate study of price supports. The OECD study depended in part that governments supply some data that were not available as well as estimates for some types of support that are probably understated for some countries.

The OECD (2001c) updated the data on government support to the fisheries sector in member countries to include data on support programs in 1998 and 1999. The data for each member country were again broken down by types of programs. However, some countries (Belgium, Netherlands, Mexico and Poland) did not provide data on government transfers for either year, and Australia, Canada and Turkey did not provide date for 1999. Given the past levels of support by Canada and Mexico in particular, the lacunae in the 1998 and 1999 data could increase significantly the provisional totals for OECD countries for those years.

The second major international source of data on fisheries subsidies is the study commissioned by the APEC Fisheries Working Group (PricewaterhouseCoopers, 2000). It is accompanied by a detailed inventory of all identifiable programs, including infrastructure and management services, in 19 of the 21 APEC member states, including programmes of eight Chinese maritime provinces. Many programs reported, however, are not accompanied by any cost data, or the data are not specific as to the year being reported. A significant difference between the APEC and OECD data is that the former covers programs that support aquaculture as well as marine capture fisheries. Aquaculture subsidies account for 30% of the total of USD 12.6 billion in subsidies estimated by the authors, leaving a total of USD 8.9 billion for capture fisheries. In addition, the APEC study also includes subsidies to processing industries, which it puts at USD 0.7 billion annually. So the total of subsidies to the maritime harvest sector is estimated to be USD 8.2 billion. Despite the absence of tabulated national totals, and of any reported or estimated costs for many of the programs, reasonably credible national estimates for five non-OECD APEC countries (Chinese Taipei, Peru, Indonesia, Malaysia and Vietnam), ranging from USD 28 million to USD 279 million annually, can be extracted from the detailed inventory in the APEC study. The inventory also provides a more reliable estimate of Mexico's subsidies than what was reported to the OECD. On the other hand, China reported only USD 44 million in infrastructure-related programs at the national level, and Chile did not report any subsidy programs at all, both of which seem unlikely.

Milazzo (1998) constructed subsidy estimates that included off-budget programs — i.e. loans and tax breaks-for five major fishing countries (Japan, Norway, United States, Russia and China) as well as the European Community. Among the programs identified by Milazzo that were omitted from the other two studies is a Japanese loan-subsidy programme for which no figures are officially published. Milazzo found that the programme represented USD 3.7 billion annually, whereas the OECD figure for total Japanese assistance to investment and modernisation is only USD 26 million in 1996 and USD 21 million in 1997.

The USD 3.7 billion figure presumably represents the portfolio of subsidised loans being financed by Japan, and the figure of USD 26 million represents the annual total for actual interest subsidies. Technically, only the latter is the actual subsidy. In this case, the loan portfolio itself is probably a better guide to the impact of the subsidy than the interest subsidies themselves. Loans to fisheries investment can leverage a significant proportion of the new investment in a fishery, particularly when the industry is in financial straits, as it was in the 1990s. Much of the USD 3.7 billion portfolio of loans represents fishing investments that would not otherwise have been made. This is particularly true when the government has a history of forgiving fisheries loans, as Japan did in the 1990s (Porter, 1998c). It would also be important to know what loan guarantee programs Japan has operated alongside this portfolio of subsidized loans, because such programs also leverage much higher borrowing by the fishing industry (Milazzo 1998; Porter, 1998c).

Milazzo also noted that the United States pays for the cost of access so that its tuna purse-seine fleet may fish under a multilateral agreement with Pacific Island states, which are not financed by the Fisheries Service but by the Department of State. The United States does not acknowledge that these payments are a subsidy that is directly linked to its fishing rights under the agreement, so it has not been notified to the WTO or included in US reporting to OECD.

WTO notifications have so far provided data on only a small proportion of total fisheries subsidies programmes that should have been notified. Furthermore, many notifications do not even indicate their cost or value to the fishing industry (Schorr, 1998; Schorr, 2001; World Wildlife Fund, 2001). Even so, these WTO notifications have provided the only official documentation on certain off-budget programs, such as a Japanese program from 1991 through 1996 that granted an additional capital depreciation to fishing vessels beyond what was allowed in the tax code for other sectors. It was unclear from the way the programme was described in the notification, however, whether the amount (USD 4.2 billion in 1996) referred to the net value of the tax break to the fishing industry, to the capital investment qualifying for the measure, or to something else. Japan has stated in its comments on an earlier draft of this study that the USD 4.2 billion refers to the "total fishery production value of the fisheries that are covered by this tax scheme." This confusion surrounding this program underlines the need for greater clarity in the presentation of tax subsidies as well as lending subsidies in WTO notifications.

The World Wildlife Fund (WWF, 2001) has attempted to provide an overall picture of total subsidies worldwide by combining and correlating OECD, APEC and WTO data. Juxtaposing the two major studies and the limited WTO data and subtracting where needed to avoid double-counting is a useful exercise; but the adjusted totals from the three sources for 1996 and 1997 in the WWF study do not add up. WWF's reorganisation of the APEC inventory makes it easy to add up country-by-country totals for those programmes with quantitative values in the original APEC document. However, these totals are much smaller in most cases than the actual country-by-country estimates made by the APEC researchers, which were required in order to derive overall APEC totals by category of assistance.

The WWF study concludes that the one Japanese program of tax concessions to its fleets, which had never been reported to the OECD, and which does not appear in the APEC study, increases the amount of documented subsidies for global capture fisheries by more than 50%. WWF questions whether the combined figures now available come close to capturing the actual global total, suggesting that the total is at least USD 15 billion annually. As noted above, this total depends on including the USD 4.2 billion attributed to the Japanese tax subsidy program, which remains to be clarified.

Some additional data on fisheries subsidies are available from national, sub-national and EU websites. Steenblik and Wallis (2001) report on websites that provide detailed information on the support programs of Germany, the Netherlands, Portugal, Australia, Canada, Mexico, New Zealand and the United States. In some cases, these data may yield some details that are not covered in the OECD study; in others (*e.g.* Mexico and the US), they do not appear to cover all of the state's programs, some of which are administered by other agencies.

## *Methodologies for measuring potential environmental benefits of subsidy reform*

Thus far, no methodology has been used to predict the impact of a change in the level or the distribution of different types of subsidies to a given national fisheries sector on the state of the fish stocks in the fishery. A recent FAO Expert Consultation (FAO, 2000) suggests two quantitative approaches aimed at estimating the impacts of subsidies on the sustainability of fish stocks: "dynamic mathematical modelling using real fishery data" and "econometric estimation of relationships based on time series, cross section or pooled data." The participants in the consultation noted the need to trace the effects of subsidies on costs and revenue and thus industry profits, and then to link changes in profits statistically to changes in fishing effort.

The FAO Committee on Fisheries agreed at its February 2001 meeting that the Fisheries Department should continue to investigate the nature and effect of subsidies on fisheries sector and called for a second Expert Consultation on subsidies. The current work program of the Fisheries Department calls for this consultation to focus on the impact of subsidies on the economic activities of recipients, based on empirical research using a common methodology. Meanwhile, the Fisheries Department itself is conducting surveys of the profitability of selected fisheries around the world, which are intended to help establish the role that subsidies play in profitability (FAO, 2001).

In the absence of experience with quantitative methods for linking the type and size of subsidy with changes in the level of fishing capacity in the fishing fleet, case studies offer a way of characterising the effects of certain types of subsidy under certain conditions. A number of case studies of fisheries subsidies provided by OECD countries and the European Community from the 1960's through 1980s illustrate the fact that, in fisheries that are still in the phase of rapidly growing capitalisation, the provision of subsidies, especially for capital costs, does have a pronounced impact on the rate of capacity growth (Porter 1998c; OECD, 2000a). In some cases, the relationship between subsidies and capacity expansion has been so close that the bulk of the capacity increase during a given period can be attributed to subsidies rather than to the effect of open access common pool character of the fishery. For example, Flaaten and Wallis (2000) found a strong positive statistical correlation between the level of interest transfers provided by the National Fishery Bank in Norway and the number of newly built vessels entering the fleet during the 1980s. By the second half of the 1990s, most OECD countries had redirected most of their financial transfers, apart from basic services, to the objective of capacity reduction.

It is not clear how many of the world's fisheries have reached the point at which total costs associated with fishing are greater than fishing industry revenues. Even after the equilibrium point has been reached, however, it appears that the perverse incentive inherent in the absence of property rights continues to push up or at least maintain the level of fishing effort. Standard economic models of the fishery (Gordon, 1954; Clark and Munro, 1975) were based on the implicit assumption that fleet capital is perfectly "malleable". In fact, however, fleet capital is relatively "non-malleable" — *i.e.* it cannot be easily adapted for use in another marine industry (*e.g.* freight transport) in response to price signals (Clark *et al.*, 1979; Munro, 1999). In addition, because of the high fixed costs of entry into the industry, vessel owners tend to remain in the industry as long as they can recover operating costs, even if they don't earn a satisfactory return on total investment (FAO, 1993).

As fisheries go from the stage of being under-exploited to the stages of being fully exploited and finally overexploited, the relationships among subsidy levels, the levels of fishing fleet capacity, and the state of fish stocks also change. Fleet over-capacity (defined as capacity above the level required for maximum sustainable yield) has existed in virtually every major fishing fleet for some years (Porter, 1998a). By the 1990s, the capacity of most major states' fishing fleets had begun to level off, and growth has continued to take place at a much slower rate compared with previous decades (Greboval, 1999).

In fisheries that already suffer from severe over-capacity, the primary issue in regard to the impact of fisheries subsidies is no longer whether they *increase* the level of over-capacity and overexploitation of resources, but whether they impede the process of adjustment to the economic conditions accompanying over-capacity. In general the removal of subsidies should increase the costs of fishing for the vessel owners in a given fishery, thus making unprofitable some vessels that were previously profitable. However, the very limited malleability of capital in the fisheries sector will limit the effect of subsidy removal on the level of capacity. In highly over-capitalised fisheries, even if subsidy removal does result in withdrawal of some vessels from the fishery, it is likely to remove only the least profitable vessels from its fisheries, and allow the remaining capacity to concentrate on the most profitable fishery. Thus subsidy removal will not necessarily alleviate the pressure on stocks (Vestergaard, Squires and Kirkley, 1999).

Case study evidence can also help assess whether and in what circumstances subsidies for the specific purpose of reducing capacity can bring about an improvement in the state of stocks or a lasting reduction in fleet capacity. Reviews of a number of case studies on subsidies for capacity reduction through vessel or license buy-outs (OECD, 1995; Gates *et al.*, 1997; Holland *et al.*, 1999; OECD, 2000a; Porter, 2002) indicate that they can reduce capacity in the short run, but that those remaining in the fishery tend to increase their capacity or effort, or both, in response, as long as the basic economic structure of the fishery remains distorted by the absence of property rights. The subsequent increases in capacity are often in the form of technological improvement rather than additional vessels.

The case study literature suggests that the impact of a given type of fishery subsidy on fish stocks through changes in the profitability of a given level of capacity and effort thus depend on the incentive structure and management characteristics of the specific fishery (*i.e.* whether the fishery is distorted by a "race to the fish" and how effectively the management system constrains catch and effort) and on the degree of over-capacity in that fishery. A matrix approach that takes into account all of the relevant characteristics of the fishery would facilitate the systematic assessment of the environmental consequences of subsidy introduction or removal (Porter, 2002).

## Data gaps and additional research needed

Despite three overlapping major data sources (OECD, APEC and WTO), a few gaps in the data on financial transfers in significant fishing states remain to be filled. Tax subsidies and subsidised lending programmes could be better documented than they have been in OECD and WTO reporting. Major gaps also exist in the information reported for non-OECD countries. For example, data collected so far on Chile and for China appear not to be complete.

In order to use economic models or linear programming to establish the impacts of adding or withdrawing subsidies on economic decisions regarding fleet capacity and effort, researchers will need detailed data on fixed and variable costs to the fishing industry in various countries. Variable cost data need not be based on a survey of many fishing companies but can be compiled from random samples of vessels in the fishery, and vessel prices can be gleaned from public advertisements (Squires, Alauddin and Kirkley, 1994). A relatively small number of case studies in certain countries would make this research task more manageable.

In the search for evidence, either from empirical research or modelling exercises, that subsidy removal can bring about a reduction in the level of fishing effort, it would make sense to begin with cases that involve those combinations of subsidy types and fisheries most likely to demonstrate such a supply response. Thus the FAO Committee on Fisheries has decided to focus on cases such as subsidies to distant water fleets, the fisheries of third countries and under-exploited fisheries (FAO, 2001), where the sensitivity of vessel owners to a change in profitability is likely to be greatest.

Given the importance of subsidies for vessel buy-backs, more systematic work analyzing the record of past and present programs with a similar framework to assess the relationship between various conditions and results would make a valuable contribution to understanding the problem. Case studies that can be aggregated and compared could include updated information on programmes that have been previously studied. Particularly important is the adoption of a common methodology for gauging changes in fishing capacity and the health of fish stocks from the baseline to later years.

A major issue raised by fisheries economists regarding vessel buy-backs is the "moral hazard" problem. They argue that, if vessel owners have reason to believe that a first vessel buy-back program will be followed others in the future, they will adjust their behavior to take full advantage of the opportunity (Gates et al, 1997a; Arnason, 1999; Munro, 1999, OECD, 2000a; Munro and Sumaila, 2001). This is an insight from economics which provides a strong hypothesis that should be verified in countries that have undertaken vessel buy-backs. No such empirical research appears to have been done.

# Forests

## *General characteristics of the sector*

- In much of the world outside the OECD, forests exploited by commercial logging companies are owned by states, which raises issues of resource under-pricing and resource rents.

- Roads and other infrastructure provided by states represent costs that logging firms would have to pay if the forests were on private land, either directly or through the fee paid to the owner for logging rights.

- Important linkages often exist between the processing sector and overexploitation by the production sector, through vertical integration and export restrictions on raw logs.

## *Defining and measuring forest subsidies*

Three general types of subsidies have been widely recognised in the literature as having been provided to producers of forest products: budgetary subsidies for road-building or other services of value to the sector; resource rent subsidies inherent in provision of access to public forests at costs below the commercial value of the resource; and quantitative restrictions on timber exports or high log-export taxes, which benefit wood processing industries. Subsidies to the wood processing industry may be included in calculations of subsidy to the forest sector, because of the high degree of vertical integration between timber companies and sawmilling and plymilling industries in many countries and potential impacts on the state of the forest.

Net budgetary subsidies can be calculated by comparing budgetary outlays that benefit forest companies with revenues from those companies for government services. It is often complicated — though by no means impossible — to determine precisely what programs should be counted as benefiting the timber industry, as illustrated by the cases of the United States, Canada and Australia referred to below. Input price subsidies for the wood processing industry are estimated by calculating the difference between domestic log prices for wood processing industry and some reference price for the same logs. The subsidy from failure to capture full economic rents on timber is calculated as the amount of the "stumpage value" of the timber, or the value of the timber that is solely attributable to market demand for the good rather than to any cost of production, that is not captured by the state.

Resource-rent subsidies may be provided when states give concessions to logging firms to cut timber in state-owned forests and collect royalties that represent less than the commercial value of the timber in the concession. The resource-rent subsidy is calculated by subtracting the total cost of bringing the timber to market, including all forest charges and the cost of attracting the necessary investment, from the total stumpage value of the timber (Repetto, 1988; Day, 1998). In the case of Canadian softwood lumber, as many as four different methods have been used to calculate the stumpage value (Gale *et al.*, 1999). Some have suggested that one of the costs of production that should be included in calculations of stumpage value is the cost of forest regeneration, maintenance and protection (NIEIR, 1996; Ruzicka and Moura Costa, 1997). In many countries where regulation of forest concessions is weak, however, logging companies generally fail to carry out these basic services. Road-building is a cost of production, but would not be subtracted in calculating stumpage value if roads used by the logging firm are built and paid for by the state.

## *Country-by-country forest subsidy data available*

No inter-governmental or non-governmental organisation has systematically collected data on government transfers to forest industries on a global or regional basis. However, some efforts have been made by government and non-government analysts to estimate these subsidies for certain countries. The World Resources Institute (WRI) has analyzed data on transfers to the forest sector in the United States. The WRI study asserts that the accounting methods used by the US Forest Service have systematically minimised its losses in selling timber from national forests to logging companies; accordingly, its analysis estimated that this program operated at an average annual net loss during the fiscal years 1993-1997 of USD 307.5 million (Sizer, 2000). Another independent study, using a cash flow analysis of Forest Service data (Oppenheimer, 2001), estimated the net loss in 1998 as being USD 407 million.

According to a critical study sponsored by the Sierra Club of Canada (Gale *et al.*, 1999), foregone budget and tax expenditures from the Canadian Government benefiting the logging and processing industries totalled approximately CAD 400 million in 1997. Transfers to the forest industry from the British Columbia Provincial Government for the same year, according to the same study, appear to have totalled about CAD 2.51 billion. The study may overestimate the level of subsidies by the Provincial government. Of this amount, CAD 1.73 billion was accounted for by the estimated resource rent subsidy, which is the median of an extrapolation from four quite disparate methodologies. The study lists ten separate British Columbia Provincial

Government programmes as subsidies, but only two of these appear to be actual transfers to the industry. The analysis includes all public administration costs of the Ministry of Forests and the Ministry of Environment, Lands and Parks, for example, as "forgone expenditures" (Gale *et al.*, 1999).

Australia's States have direct responsibility for forest management under the Australian Federal/State system. A 1996 study, sponsored by the Australian government (NIEIR, 1996) and aimed at estimating the total level of Australian forest subsidies, found that it was not possible to determine precisely how much of reported spending by State governments could be attributed directly to forestry operations, and how much had a public goods aspect. Based on an analysis of the State of Victoria alone, the study suggested that total Australian financial subsidies to forestry operations could have been in the neighbourhood of AUD 100 million, but might well be higher.[7]

Statistics on subsidies provided by the EU to the forest industries in its members states are incomplete, but a study of the 1994-2000 period estimated that the total of these subsidies was more than EUR 2.5 billion (*i.e.* EUR 416 million annually), and that half of that sum was spent on afforestation programmes (Toivonen *et al.*, 1999; Toivonen, 2001).

Finland has traditionally provided substantial budgetary support to its forest industry, and a recent study (Leppanen *et al.*, 2001) estimates that the level of financial support for that industry has been at roughly ECU 50 million annually, mainly in the form of grants for regeneration, since 1995. The same study estimates the "effective rate of assistance" (defined as the proportion of net assistance to the unassisted value added to the industry) at only about 1-2%. A compilation of studies on individual European countries (Ottitsch *et al.*, 2001) provides official data on government financial transfers to the forest sector in the Czech Republic, Poland, Slovenia and Estonia as of 1999-2000.

The only estimates for forest subsidies across a large number of countries are for resource rent subsidies. The most comprehensive study of the subject (Day, 1998) provides estimates of subsidies either in absolute values or percentages of total available resource rents - or both - for 17 tropical forest countries and two boreal forest countries (Canada-British Columbia and Russia). The data includes estimates for a date in the 1990s in nearly every case. However, the data is drawn from other published sources, and the author warns that the studies cited are not necessarily comparable in methodology and types of data collected. Some studies include fee evasion as part of the estimate, for example, while others do not.

Another study (Contreras-Hermosilla, 2000) reviews estimates for nine tropical forest countries, including three countries not covered in Day (1998), for years ranging from 1989 to 1997. In the country surveys, only Malaysia collected more than 30% of the potential rents. In addition to the 28 countries cited in these two studies, estimates of resource rent subsidies have been calculated for various years or periods from the 1970s to the early 1990s for Gabon (Repetto, 1988), the Ivory Coast and Guinea (Grut, Gray and Egli, 1991). Resource-rent subsidies in Peninsular Malaysia have been estimated for different periods by several authors (Vincent, 1990; Gillis, 1988b; Vincent and Hadi, 1993). Mohd Shawahid et al., (1997) calculates that the State government has captured 20% of the total resource rent, but that it could capture 80% of that rent by using a tender system for allocating concessions. Estimates of resource-rent subsidies have also been developed for Canada for the early and late-1970s (Schwindt, 1987) and for the 1990s (Gale et al., 1999). An Australian study estimated the under-pricing of hardwood and pulpwood logs through low royalty rates in two states (Marsden Jacobs, 2001). Thus estimates in regard to failure to collect all potential rents on the resource have been attempted for a total of 27 countries, although not, unfortunately, for the same years. Although it does not estimate resource-rent subsidies, a study by Vincent and Casteneda (1997) estimates resource rents for roundwood production in fourteen Asian countries, which could be compared with total timber royalties for the same countries to estimate resource rent subsidies.

Log export restrictions have been utilised as a means of supporting domestic wood processing industries in at least 13 countries since the late 1980s. An earlier report (LEEC, 1993) listed nine tropical timber countries that had imposed either bans or quantitative restrictions or high export taxes on log exports as of 1989. Scattered estimates of price-support subsidies to wood processing industries have come from case studies of log export restrictions or bans or high export taxes, or both, on raw logs in Canada, Indonesia, Malaysia, Ghana, Ecuador, Bolivia and Costa Rica. The U.S. Department of Commerce (1993) alleged that the log export ban instituted by British Columbia and some other timber-producing provinces was providing a subsidy to the Canadian softwood lumber industry estimated at roughly 8% of the value of Canada's softwood lumber exports. In the Indonesian case, the price of logs in the early 1990s, both under a complete log export ban and high export taxes that replaced it, was only about half the world price when sold to a processor independent of the logger but far less than that when the plywood operations were affiliated with the logging company (Varangis et al., 1991; World Bank, 1993). Others have estimated that the Ecuadorian and Bolivian processing industries obtained logs at only 15% to 40% of what they would have paid in the absence of the log ban, and the Costa Rican processing industry could purchase logs at 18-52% of the world price (Kishor et al., 2001; Simula, 1999).

*Methodologies for estimating the potential environmental effects of subsidy reform*

Researchers at the Finnish Forest Research Institute have published a study on the impact of public support for forestry on timber supply (Leppanen *et al.*, 2001b), which may provide a research methodology for relating at least the rate of timber production to the level of support. Unfortunately, the paper could not be obtained during the time period of this study. No other methodology for measuring the impact of budgetary support to timber companies on forest health could be found in the literature.

As is the case with other sectors, subsidies are not the primary cause of unsustainable management of forest resources. The most important factor in the damage done to the forest by logging is the logging techniques used. And those techniques depend on other incentive measures, including greater stability and transferability of tenure and specific economic rewards for managing the resource for long-term sustainability, than on collection of adequate royalties (Paris and Ruzicka, 1991; Ruzicka and Moura Costa, 1997). Eliminating resource-rent subsidies, therefore, cannot by itself induce the concessionaire to exploit forests in a sustainable manner. Nevertheless, some resource economists have argued that the failure of governments to collect full economic rents on timber under-prices the resource to the logging firm and provides perverse incentives to log forests less efficiently than under adequate forest charges (Ruzicka, 1979; Repetto, 1988; Vincent and Binkley, 1992; Gray, 1996 and 1997).

Whether the collection of full resource rents can reduce the area harvested, or the intensity of the harvesting, however, has been the subject of intense debate. One view is that the extent of harvesting cannot be influenced by the level of resource rents collected, because cutting all the trees within the concession would still be profitable even without windfall profits (Day, 1998). However, other economists have argued that the imposition of adequate royalties on the logger increases the average and marginal cost of production, and that some trees with less favourable locations would become unprofitable to harvest (Ruzicka, 1979; Paris and Ruzicka, 1991; Ruzicka and Moura Costa, 1997).

The one empirical study of the relationship between royalty levels and cutting patterns (Amacher *et al.*, 2001) concluded on the basis of research in Peninsular Malaysia that harvesting rates on high-value species are more price and royalty elastic than are harvesting rates on low-value species. They estimate that the harvest on high-value species could increase as much as 5-10% for every USD 100 decrease in the royalty payment. Under-pricing of raw logs for domestic processing industries through log-export restrictions has the effect of reducing the efficiency with which the processing industry uses the logs as well as increasing its demand for the logs. In the Indonesian case, observers have estimated that the wood-processing industry was as much as 15-20% less efficient in turning raw logs into lumber and other wood products than the most efficient processors in Asia, meaning that 15-20% more trees had to be cut than would have been the case had the logs been processed elsewhere in Asia (Constantino, 1990; Gillis, 1988a). Similarly, the protected peninsular Malaysian processing industry has been assessed as consuming between 5% and 15% more trees per unit of sawn wood than unprotected competing processing industries (Vincent and Binkley, 1992). However, these studies have not made clear what empirical evidence supported the estimates.

Case studies have also shown that the under-pricing of raw logs results in a pronounced tendency toward over-capacity in the processing industry (Barbier *et al.*, 1995; Dean, 1995; Varangis *et al.*, 1993) because it transfers revenues from log producers to the wood-processing industry. Over-capacity in the processing industry by itself does not cause overexploitation of forests, but it is likely to increase the pressure on government to increase the total allowable cut. The artificial depression of prices of raw logs also depresses the supply of logs, but only if the harvesting and processing are not integrated. When the same companies control both harvesting and processing, as is often the case, the low prices for logs as domestic inputs also translates into greater supply for the processing industry. The higher the price-elasticity of demand for logs as domestic inputs, the greater will be the increase in the demand for logs (Dean, 1995).

The Indonesian case illustrates the effect on the rate of harvesting of under-pricing logs through a log-export ban. According to a study by an Indonesian NGO, the artificially low domestic prices of the logs and sawn wood had created significant overcapacity in wood processing industries, pushing processing capacity well beyond the maximum sustainable level of cut, which was then followed by unsustainable levels of logging (WALHI, 1991; World Bank, 1993). The upward pressure on harvesting levels was exerted not only by the price of logs but also by the absence of any effective control over concessionaires and the opportunity to capture export markets for plywood throughout Asia by underpricing competitors and then raising prices (Dauvergne, 1997). Ecuador's log ban has also been shown to have encouraged unsustainable rates of cutting by creating much greater demand for logs for the processing industry (Southgate and Whitaker, 1992). These qualitative analyses of the linkage between log export restrictions, over-capacity, and over-exploitation of forests cannot easily be translated, however, into quantitative research methodologies.

*Data gaps and additional research needed*

No comparable data on government transfers to the forest sector for similar years have been collected for OECD countries or for other groups of countries. The data that are available have not yet been consolidated in a single database, nor has any attempt been made to validate the data, nor to correlate it in terms of countries and periods covered. Nor has anyone compared the methodologies used to estimate forest subsidies based on program aggregation in the OECD countries. A synthesis and analysis of all the available data would be a useful exercise in the absence of a more systematic collection effort.

No quantitative methodology appears to have been used to estimate the environmental impacts of subsidy reform in the forest sector, except for the correlation analysis done by Amacher *et al.* (2001) to determine how rates of cutting of high-value and lower-value species change with royalty rates. That correlation is not quite the same as a correlation between resource rent-subsidy rates and cutting rates. It would be useful to explore whether the data exist to correlate different levels of resource-rent subsidy and cutting rates on high-value species or all species in the same forest areas. The inefficiency effect of export restrictions also remains to be studied systematically through collection and analysis of empirical evidence. This would require a researcher to obtain historical data from companies in countries with such export restrictions on the amount of timber consumed in ply-milling and saw-milling operations per common unit of output as well as similar data from companies in countries without export restrictions.

## Energy

*General characteristics of the sector*

- Fossil fuels (coal, petroleum, natural gas) and electricity-generating technologies, are traded in regional or world markets, whereas most electricity is usually traded on domestic, but not international, markets.

- The competing energy sources have widely differing environmental implications, so the technology effect is one of the most important aspects of the environmental impacts of subsidies and their removal.

*Defining and measuring energy subsidies*

The International Energy Agency (1999) has defined an energy subsidy as any government action that:

- lowers the cost of energy production,
- raises the price received by energy producers, or
- lowers the price paid by energy consumers.

The IEA identified four major forms of energy subsidies: grants and credits (soft loans or interest-rate subsidies) to producers or consumers of energy; market price support (*e.g.* through regulatory requirements to purchase a given amount of fuel from a specific source at a regulated price or price controls to promote supply and consumption of particular energy sources); differential tax rates on different fuels; and publicly-funded research and development programs. Although these have very different impacts on energy markets, and on the environment, aggregating totals for these forms of subsidy provides a rough estimate of the magnitude of government intervention in the energy sector.

Several studies (*e.g.* OECD, 1997b) have focussed only on market price support to producers or, more commonly, on market transfers to consumers. In either case, they have measured the difference between actual prices and reference prices that would obtain in an undistorted market. This definition is not necessarily inconsistent with the first, but focuses only on the net effect of measures on the "price gap". Subsidies that allow producers to stay in business while selling their coal or some other product at a world price are not picked up. The reference price, which is a measure of the true market value of a unit of energy, is the opportunity cost of its consumption. It is represented by either the border price for internationally traded energy products or the cost of production for non-traded ones, adjusted for transport and distribution costs. The resulting estimate of the price gap is sensitive to the choice of exchange rate used to convert local currencies into a common currency. Both official exchange rates and exchange rates based on purchasing power parities have advantages and disadvantages, and both the OECD and the IEA have chosen to use official exchange rates in the past.

As originally conceived in the energy literature (Kosmo, 1987), the price gap method was applied only to measure subsidies that reduce the end-use price of energy, omitting from consideration those subsidies that actually raise the price of energy to the user. That was because the focus of much of the original work was on developing countries and countries in transition, where under-pricing of energy is rife. However, in developed countries certain high-cost energy industries have been protected from foreign competition. For example, in western Europe, coal producers who cannot compete against imported coal have been supported, primarily by requiring purchases at an official price that is significantly above the world reference price (and thus, in effect, taxing consumers of steam coal), supplemented by direct payments to producers (Steenblik and Coryonnakis, 1995). The OECD (2001d) calculated both subsidies that reduced end-use prices to below a world reference price and subsidies from consumers and taxpayers to producers that raised end-use prices above the reference price. The result was a country-by-country comparison in which "consumer price wedges" and "producer price wedges" were distinguished.

The calculation of price wedges is based on a reference price for fossil fuels that are traded internationally. For energy that is not traded internationally, such as most electricity and certain types of coal, a substitute reference price has to be constructed based on the cost of production. If data on the long-run marginal costs of production are not available, average production costs are estimated (World Bank, 1997).

### Country-by-country energy subsidy data available

Estimates of support for coal are more systematic and complete than for other forms of energy. Indeed, the only regular, systematic reporting of energy subsidies carried out by an international body is the IEA's annual estimation of PSEs for coal. These estimates were first produced in 1988, originally for five IEA member countries (IEA, 1988) — generally showing PSEs back to 1982 — and were later updated in the IEA's annual review of *Energy Policies of IEA Countries* (1989-2001). More recently, the IEA's annual statistical bulletin, *Coal Information* (IEA, 2002) has provided annual PSE estimates for coal production in France, Germany, Japan, Spain, Turkey and UK for 1991 though 2001, including calculations of aid per tonne of coal equivalent in local currency and in US dollars. It also distinguishes among specific subsidy programmes that benefit current production, programmes that do not benefit current production, and programmes to promote industry contraction for each of the six counties from 1990 through 2001.

The IEA also maintains a database on annual country-by-country expenditures for energy research and development for the years 1974-2000. Some partial information on subsidies is provided in its in-depth reviews of the energy policies of IEA member countries. Over the four-year period from 1998 through 2001, the IEA published detailed reviews of 25 IEA member countries. In 2002, the IEA also published a review of Russia's energy policies. The reviews usually include data on some aspect of energy subsidies in the country. In some cases (Turkey and Russia, for example), the reviews provide data on support to the coal industry; in others (Spain, for example) they provide data on support for renewable energy technologies. None of these reviews appears to provide a complete analysis of energy subsidies provided by the country, however.

The European Commission's Directorate for Competition maintains a database on "state aid" (*i.e.* government transfers) to a limited number of sectors, including support provided by EU Member states for coal mining and for the general objective of "energy savings". Country-by-country data on these two categories of expenditure are provided for the years 1997 through 1999 in its second edition of *State Aid Scoreboard*.

Apart from these continuing exercises, the IEA, the OECD and the World Bank have all at different times tried to estimate market-price support to producers or market transfers to energy consumers in OECD or non-OECD countries. Based only on consumer price gaps, the World Bank (1997) estimated price-wedge subsidies for petroleum products, natural gas and coal for 17 non-OECD countries for 1990-91 and 1995-96. More-detailed data on which the calculations were based can be found in another study prepared for the World Bank (Rajkumar, 1996). These estimates of developing countries and former socialist countries in transition were presented only as "orders of magnitude", because the data on which they were based were of relatively poor quality.

Using the price-gap approach, the IEA (1999) developed estimates of energy subsidies (market transfers) in eight non-OECD countries (China, Russian Federation, India, Indonesia, Iran, South Africa, Venezuela, Khazakhstan) chosen because of their high levels of total energy consumption as of 1997-98. The studies found that energy prices in those countries were on average 20% below reference prices.

The OECD's Joint Working Party on Trade and Environment (OECD, 2001d) estimated both market-price support to producers and market transfers to consumers of fossil fuels as of 1996 for 26 OECD countries, as well as the average for all EEC member countries. These data represented weighted averages of price wedges for coal, natural gas, heavy fuel oil and light fuel oil. The same study also estimated fossil-fuel price gaps for Brazil, China, the former Soviet Union and India.

Ruijgrok and Oosterhuis (1997) estimated budgetary support for fossil fuels, nuclear energy, electricity, renewable energy and conservation for all

15 EU member states, Norway and Switzerland as of 1995. The authors quantify only direct payments and tax expenditures from state budgets that lower the cost of energy production, consumption or conservation, while acknowledging that indirect subsidies in the form of soft loans, provision of infrastructure and limiting liability for energy firms in the event of nuclear accident are also important. They find that 22% of these budgetary subsidies were going towards supporting renewable energy and conservation. The study does not attempt to relate the totals for direct subsidies to end-use prices or production costs, but it does compare the European countries according to the rate of subsidisation in dollars per TOE (tons of oil equivalent) of final energy demand.

Some governments provide data on budgetary expenditures for energy on websites related to their national budgets, which are useful to varying degrees in estimating total subsidies to the energy sector. Three such websites were found in the course of this study. Of these three, for Japan, provides one of the most convenient guides to its energy expenditures, showing the breakdown of its expenditures among measures to support domestic coal, oil development and stockpiling, new energy and conservation and nuclear power.

The Australian government's total expenditures on fuel and energy for fiscal year 2000-2001 and projections for such spending through fiscal year 2004-2005. New Zealand's expenditures for energy and for conservation and renewable energy resources are shown in the Detailed Statement of Appropriations of its 2000-2001 budget document on the website of its national treasury.

In two studies, the US Department of Energy's Energy Information Administration (EIA) calculated US subsidies to energy markets in the United Sates, based only on budgetary expenditures as of 1999. One study (EIA, 1999) analysed assistance to primary energy industries (including renewable energy and electricity); the other (EIA, 2000) analysed assistance to energy transformation and end use. The EIA identified nearly USD 4 billion in subsidies to primary energy in 1999, of which 60% were tax expenditures and virtually all of the remainder for research, development and demonstration. For energy transformation and end-use subsidies, it identified USD 2.2 billion, of which 63% was accounted for by direct expenditures.[8]

However, an independent study focusing on US subsidies to the oil industry alone (Koplow and Martin, 1998) calculated that tax expenditures benefiting the oil industry totalled USD 1.8 to USD 3.68 billion in 1995. Since tax expenditures for all forms of energy had fallen from USD 2.2 billion to USD 1.7 billion, according to EIA figures, the detailed comparison of the methodologies used in the two studies would be useful. Koplow and Martin estimated the total budgetary subsidy to oil alone, excluding defence expenditures that they relate to oil, but including the costs of the US strategic petroleum reserve, at between USD 4.5 billion and USD 10.9 billion.

A detailed study of Australia's direct budgetary and tax expenditures for fossil fuel production and consumption (Riedy, 2001) covers direct payments and tax expenditures and includes expenditures by state governments. The study includes some categories that would be more properly considered under transport as well as some that are arguably not transfers to industry or to consumers.

## *Methodologies for quantifying the environmental impacts of subsidy reform*

One methodology for estimation of the impacts of energy subsidies would be to look at the impact of each type of subsidy on emissions separately, and then analyse any interactions among them. Steenblik and Coroyannakis (1995) and Newberry (1995) note that for coal, it is crucial to establish in the case of a particular subsidy whether the output is secured through purchase obligations, as ending those obligations could have the effect of reducing coal consumption through substitution effects, even if it contributes to overall higher energy consumption.

Several qualitative analyses of the effects of a reduction or removal of specific forms of subsidies to energy, summarised by Vollebergh (1999), support the generalisation that removing subsidies to the long-run marginal cost of a fuel technology are especially important to long-term emissions, because power-plant investment decisions are strongly affected by the relative prices of alternative technologies. They also provide evidence to show that withdrawing support to industrial consumers is more effective at reducing emissions than withdrawing the same amount of support to households.

Another method that has been used for economies in which the subsidy consists of a consumer price wedge, is to calculate the percentage change in prices that would occur with subsidy removal (derived by dividing the price gap by the reference price) and then using data on the elasticity of demand to estimate the change in consumption that would result from an elimination of the price gap (IEA, 1999). Price elasticities of energy demand vary, but a number of studies have found that long-run elasticities for energy demand tend to be around -0.5 (World Bank, 1997). The resulting estimate for reduced energy consumption can then be converted into estimates of reduced

71

emissions by using relevant functions for carbon dioxide and other pollutants per unit of energy.

The environmental benefits of eliminating coal subsidies in Western Europe cannot be estimated on the basis of lowered coal prices but must include the impact of fuel substitution as well. In some of these countries (for example, the UK following energy-market liberalisation), the substitution effect can be strong enough to outweigh the effect of the reduced price of coal on pollutant emissions (Steenblik and Coroyannakis, 1995; Haugland, 1995). In Germany, however, coal consumers are already free to choose among different fuels, so the removal of support to the domestic coal industry would presumably lead them to switch to imported coal (IEA, 2000). It is the substitution effect from coal to less-polluting fuels that would represent the greatest gain in reduced local pollutants and greenhouse gas emissions. Thus cross-elasticities of coal and of competing fuels are crucial to the calculation of results.   $\lambda$

The IEA (1999) estimated changes in carbon dioxide emissions for eight high-consuming non-OECD countries where domestic prices are on average 21% below reference prices. Comparing the baseline case and the case of an economy without energy subsidies in each country, the study estimates an average reduction in carbon emissions of 16% across the eight countries, with the reductions ranging from a high of 26% for Venezuela to a low of 8% for South Africa. However, the study was limited by the inability to estimate fuel substitution, based on cross-elasticities between the prices of different fuels, or the longer-run consumption savings from the more rapid development of energy-efficient technologies.

Most of the case studies in the environmental benefits of energy subsidy reduction have focused on greenhouse-gas emissions. However, several cases have estimated the reduction in acid emissions from elimination of subsidies to the electricity sector. These studies demonstrate that the benefits of subsidy removal for acid emissions can be proportionally greater than for carbon dioxide emissions in locations where acid emission are at levels that can cause environmental damage (OECD Annex I Working Group 1997).

Another model that has been used to estimate the impacts of a phase-out of coal subsidies is the C-Cubed model (Anderson and McKibbin, 1997). It utilizes a less complex model of world regions than the GREEN model, but has more economic sectors than the GREEN model and combines a dynamic macroeconomic modelling approach with a disaggregated, intertemporal general equilibrium model of the U.S. economy (McKibbin and Wilcoxen, 1996). In the study's simulation, the phase-out of coal subsidies in Western Europe and Japan, plus imposition of a tax on the environmental damage from coalmining, would lower OECD carbon-dioxide emissions by 13% and global carbon emissions by 5%. If the major non-OECD countries were to remove subsidies to consumers by raising domestic prices of coal to world reference levels; moreover, it would reduce their carbon emissions by 4% and total world emissions by 8% below the baseline case.

The OECD (2001d) studied the environmental effects of a multilateral agreement on liberalisation of energy trade using the OECD's General Equilibrium Environmental (GREEN) multi-country, multi-sector model devised to quantify global costs of policies aimed at reducing carbon emissions. The model simulated three scenarios involving the elimination of all price wedges and consumer taxes (prices for consumers above the world reference price): one in which only OECD countries liberalise, one in which only non-OECD countries liberalise and one in which all countries liberalise. The simulation results showed that carbon emissions in the OECD countries would increase slightly by 2010 compared with the "business as usual" scenario if only OECD countries liberalise, but would be reduced by 6.2% if all countries liberalise and 6.3% if only non-OECD countries liberalise. The simulation had several weaknesses that probably caused it to underestimate the environmental benefits of energy subsidy removal: the model was based on incomplete data on producer price wedges, covered only subsidies to industry and power generation, excluded producer-price wedges for crude oil; and probably did not fully reflect the effect of technological improvements on energy efficiency, both through its assumptions and its 2010 cut-off date.

Regardless of the model used, in order to ensure that the environmental benefits of energy subsidy reduction are estimated as accurately as possible, the simulation must take into account the effect on the redistribution of production, the world price effect and the long-term effects of fuel substitution. Since subsidy elimination in higher-cost countries would redistribute coal production to lower-cost producing countries, and the environmental effects of that increased production must also be estimated. Little work has been done in this area. However, Steenblik and Coryannakis (1995) showed that, on a tonne-for-tonne base, a shift in production from deep underground mines in Europe to shallow surface mines elsewhere would considerably reduce emissions of methane from exposed coal seams. Coal subsidy removal would also increase the level of coal imports in response to more expensive domestic coal prices, raising world prices and lowering world-wide consumption through substitution and energy efficiency (Anderson and McKibbin 1997). That could be even more significant than the reductions in response to increased world prices in the countries covered in the study (OECD 1998a). Finally, the long-term effects of coal subsidy removal (i.e. more than 20 years) should be much larger than the shorter-term effects. Case studies that estimate results only to fifteen or twenty years in the future, such as Anderson and McKibbin (1997) and DRI/McGraw Hill (1997), are likely to underestimate total benefits, because the full effects would not be felt until existing plants are obsolescent and new investments are required (OECD 1998a; OECD Annex I Export Group 1997).

### Data gaps and additional research needed

Energy sector price data are available for all OECD countries, but the data on producer price gaps even for major energy consuming non-OECD countries remains incomplete. Data on own-price and elasticity of demand and cross-elasticities are also still very quite inadequate for non-OECD countries. The IEA (1999), for example, had to rely on estimates for own-price elasticity that were often contradictory and included estimates that were outside plausible ranges.

Further simulations of multilateral agreements on phasing out all energy subsidies or coal subsidies alone are needed that incorporate more complete data on producer-price wedges, as well as the full long-term technological effects of fuel substitution in power sector investment.

## Transport

### Major characteristics of the sector

- The market for transport services is distorted by two basic structural characteristics: the significant elements of natural monopoly in the sector and its high ratios of fixed to marginal costs and high levels of sunk costs — costs that cannot be recovered by putting assets to alternative uses (ECMT, 2000; Roy, 1998).

- Competition between transport modes is a central feature of transport markets. Road transport dominates the transport market in advanced industrialised countries, accounting for 93% of all inland passenger-kilometres and 76% of all tons of freight kilometres in the ECMT countries in 1995 (ECMT 2000).

- Transport markets naturally fail in the direction of over-pricing and under-use of rail and under-pricing and over-use of roads (ECMT, 2000; Roy, 1998).

- Significant externalities in the road sector mean that marginal social costs can be far *above* average social cost. On the other hand, the very low level of externalities and increasing returns to scale in rail transportation means that marginal social costs for rail transport are far *below* average costs.

## *Defining and estimating transport subsidies*

A transport subsidy could be defined either in terms of the gap between government expenditures to transport systems and the revenues collected from those systems (cost recovery) or by the failure to internalise external costs and other marginal social costs (congestion, scarcity, accidents, operating costs) in a specific mode of transport. Another way to characterize the differences between the two definitions is that one approach uses a "full allocated cost analysis", whereas the other uses a "short-run marginal cost analysis". A recent study (Sansom *et al.*, 2001) provides the clearest delineation of the differences in relevant cost and revenue categories used by each of the two approaches.

Which definition is relevant depends on the issue to be addressed. For efficient use of infrastructure, short run marginal social cost is the relevant basis for prices. Given the increasing returns to scale in railways such prices will not always cover total costs. On the other hand, in urban areas where the inherent economies of scale in road infrastructure are accompanied by the high external costs of road use, and especially congestion, such prices will much more than cover costs. This is because infrastructure expansion is constrained by competing uses for land in cities and a resource rent arises. Fully allocated cost analysis is of more relevance to optimisation of the supply of infrastructure outside urban areas, though cost recovery is not the only or necessarily most important, criterion in determining infrastructure supply. Social cost-benefit analysis is the relevant tool for guiding policy rather than a simple pricing rule.

The 41-member European Conference of Ministers of Transport (ECMT), as well as most transport sector specialists in Europe and North America, have adopted the principle that transport prices are distorted if they fail to internalise short run marginal social costs, including the marginal costs of maintenance, reconstruction and resurfacing in the case of roads, but not other producer costs or user costs that are internalised by transport users (ECMT, 1998; Litman, 1999; ECMT, 2000; Nash, 2000).

The implication of examining transport subsidies in relation to the optimisation of infrastructure use is that main instrument of policy for dealing with perverse subsidy in the transport sector is the application of Pigouvian taxes and subsidies to reduce externalities (Button, 1994) and maximise social welfare. Cost-recovery is not part of this framework.

A large number of external costs of transport could be considered in estimating the subsidy to a particular transportation mode. The ECMT has identified the costs of noise, vibration, air pollution, accidents, greenhouse gas emissions and congestion as most relevant to these calculations (ECMT, 2000). The external costs of infrastructure provision, such as land take, landscape impact and barrier effects on wildlife and human communities are often not considered because of data deficiencies. Differences remain over how to calculate costs related to greenhouse gases: some countries have adopted a "dose-response" approach to calculating those costs, whereas others have opted "shadow values" derived from the greenhouse-gas emissions reduction obligations adopted by governments or from the EU's carbon tax proposals (Ricci and Friedrich, 1999; Nelthorpe *et al.*, 1998).

Different valuation methods are used for different categories of external costs: for costs associated with accidents, revealed preference is the preferred method in Europe; for traffic noise, it is prevention costs. For air pollution, however, European researchers have developed a more detailed, bottom-up "impact pathway" approach that has been found to be more effective in estimating the external environment costs of a mode of transport. The "impact pathway" approach uses detailed site- and technology-specific data, pollution dispersion models, and detailed information on location of receptors and exposure-response functions and finally assigns monetary values to the identified impacts in order to estimate environmental impacts of energy-related activities. The ExternE model developed initially for air emissions from electricity production is the most notable example. It is has been used in a series of research projects focusing on calculating the external costs of transport in different countries or in particular international corridors in Europe (IER, 1997; Friedrich *et al.*, 1998; Vossiniotis and Assimacopoulous, 1999; TRIP, 2000).

In view of the amount of data and time required to implement the "impact pathway" approach to estimation, the research strategy in Europe has been to construct simplified functions describing the relationships between marginal external costs and certain parameters such as road type, vehicle technology and population density from a large number of case studies which can then be used, either by aggregation or averaging, for estimates at various levels (Ricci and Friedrich, 1999). The European Commission launched a new research project in 2000 aimed at upgrading emissions factors for all transport sources and providing consistent emissions estimates in all EU member states.

Given estimates of external costs, econometric models are available to compute optimum prices for each mode of transport in any particular city or country. An EU-funded research project, TRENEN II STRAN, developed econometric models that convert data on external costs, taxes and resource costs into optimum prices (Proost *et al.*, 1998). The difference between these prices and existing prices can then be viewed as the degree of perverse subsidy in regard to the city, transport route or country in question. These models suggest that perverse subsidies be focused primarily on the consumer price for car use in urban areas at peak periods, circumstances in which only one third to one half of the full marginal social costs are covered by the price. For off-peak travel and for buses, prices are much closer or even equal to social costs.

Defining and measuring the degree of subsidy by the difference between efficient prices and existing prices might be applicable at the national level for some small countries in which relatively few prices for individual areas or routes are required. These could be averaged based on the proportion of total VMT represented by each mode. But for countries with very large territories such as the United States, Canada or Australia, it appears to be impractical to attempt to estimate the subsidy based on efficient pricing criteria at the national level. Such estimates are only meaningful at the level of transportation routes or regions.

### *Country-by-country transport subsidy data available*

Data on government spending on transport infrastructure costs and revenues from transport use across a number of countries were assembled in a 1994 study conducted for the International Union of Railway,s with the exercise repeated and published in March 2000. The data included in the study were estimated infrastructure costs for road (both passenger and freight) and for rail (both passenger and freight) for all European Union member states, Norway and Switzerland. Road network expenditure data for most of the countries in the study were lacking, however, and the estimates had to be based, therefore, on a total cost/total expenditure ratio of 1.3 from calculations for Germany and Switzerland and responses from other countries to questionnaires in the UIC study.

Based on various studies, the ECMT (2000) has estimated short- and long-run marginal costs of road and rail infrastructure use in Europe per 1 000 passenger kilometres or per tonne kilometre for several European countries.

The European Union is in the process of unifying its national transport accounts through a project called UNITE, which will provide national policymakers with the analytical tools and data for national transport accounts showing estimated external social costs for the country. The methodology for the national accounts and the marginal cost methodology for the project were established in November 2000. Pilot national transport accounts covering environmental costs and capital and maintenance costs for 1996 and 1998, are available for the UK (Sansom *et al.*, 2001), Germany and Switzerland (Linke, 2002) and should be available soon on the UNITE website for all fifteen members of the EU as well as Estonia, Hungary and Switzerland.

The European Environment Agency compiled and published figures on the external and infrastructure costs for rail and road transport for all 15 members of the European Community as of 1991 and their transport revenues for the same year, showing total social costs and total revenues in each case (EEA, 2000). The figures are presented misleadingly in terms of the "proportion of external and infrastructure costs covered by revenues". Though a more appropriate set of indicators has since been developed by the EEA they have yet to update the website.

The United States Department of Transportation's (US DOT's) Federal Highway Administration published a report in 1997 allocating highway-related costs, including all federal programs, to various types of vehicles. The report did not deal with air pollution, but an addendum published in 2000 estimated air pollution costs at USD 40 billion annually, which was about one-third lower than the EPA estimate for those same costs (US DOT, 1997; US DOT, 2000). The DOT report did not provide any estimate of global climate change-related costs from road transportation. It also considered that users internalise all congestion costs and two-thirds of auto accident costs.

The British government has published two relevant studies: Surface Transport Costs and Charges Great Britain 1998 (DETR 2001) which provides data on marginal social costs and revenues and also on fully allocated costs and revenues across the modes; Lorry Track and Environmental Costs (DETR 2000) which models road infrastructure and environmental costs for 16 categories of truck.

## *Methodologies for estimating environmental impacts of subsidy removal*

Existing research methodologies referred to in the transport policy literature do not provide any means of measuring environmental impacts of subsidy reduction in the form of reducing the gaps in cost coverage at the national or sub-national level. Changes in the use of transport systems do not depend on aggregate changes in expenditures and revenues, but on the specific relationship between transport charges and particular transport routes.

In order to estimate the environmental impacts of perverse subsidies in the transport sector — or their removal — researchers must determine how much difference efficient prices for different modes of transport would make in total transportation demand and in modal shifts in relation to inefficient prices and then use emissions functions to translate the level of transport demand into pollutant emissions. Such estimates are based on gauging the price elasticity of transport demand under various circumstances. Demand for travel is almost always inelastic, but its price elasticity tends to increase if a high quality alternative mode of transport is available at lower cost (VTPI, 2001). In some regions, even inelastic demand responses to changes in the direction of efficient pricing could represent a significant reduction in environmental externalities.

In 1998-99, a consortium of European consultants and universities, with funding from the European Commission Directorate-General for Transport, produced the first comprehensive reviews in Europe of the empirical and modelling evidence of time and cost elasticities for car travel in the Netherlands, Italy and Belgium (de Gong *et al.*, 1999; de Gong and Gunn, 2001). The studies used three national transport forecasting systems (the Dutch National Model, the Italian National Model and a model developed for the Brussels region) to model the cost elasticities of number of car trips, number of kilometres travelled by car, number of passenger trips and car passenger kilometres for the three countries. It also modelled responses to prices of transport mode choice, including both short-term and long-term responses.

A modelling exercise focused on price elasticities of mode choice (Nash, 2000) carried out by an international partnership of European research institutions modelled the effects of different pricing scenarios in five transport routes based in 2010, including an efficient pricing scenario based on estimates of price-relevant social costs. The exercise compared the results of the efficient pricing scenario with the base case pricing scenario to identify the effect of efficient pricing on mode choice. A major limitation of the model used, however, was that it assumed a fixed total travel demand, so it could not estimate impacts of such pricing on overall demand.

The results of the study showed that the impact of the efficient marginal cost pricing scenario on modal splits depend very strongly on the characteristics of the transport route in question. In the study of Lisbon's traffic, the efficient pricing scenario (which involved price increases for cars of 38-80%) reduced private car demand by 20-40%, depending on time period and valuation of externalities, whereas demand for rail increased by 12-43%, depending on the same factors. Efficient pricing scenario, however, led to only a very modest increase in modal share for rail of 7-10% in the London-Paris and London-Brussels routes, and no modal shift in low-density and low-externality inter-urban passenger routes in Finland and from Oslo to Gothenberg. In the Oslo to Gothenberg route, efficient prices actually produced a shift away from less polluting modes of bus and train to the more polluting cars and air modes.

To assess the impacts of efficient pricing on mode choice and total passenger travel, USEPA can use transport price elasticity estimates and its MOBILE model (version 5a), or California's EMFAC model, which process data on vehicle trips, miles travelled, speeds and the fleet mix and emissions characteristics of the vehicle fleet to estimate emissions by type of pollutant (Deakin and Harvey, 1996). On the basis of modelling results for transport systems serving the San Francisco, Los Angeles, Sacramento and San Diego areas, Deakin and Harvey suggest that a VMT fee of USD 0.02 per mile could be expected to reduce VMT by 4.5-6.3%, carbon dioxide emissions by 4.8-5.7% and NOx by 4.3-5.4% from the 1991 baseline.

A Study by the University of California at Davis (Rodier, Abraham and Johnston, 2001) uses a regional transport and land-use model for Sacramento to evaluate a range of transport demand management policies. It simulated the imposition of a USD 0.05 per mile VMT fee, which was derived from the low-end estimate of external costs of automobile in Delucchi (1997), and average parking surcharges of USD 2 for work trips and USD 1 for other trips. The total charges represented a 30% increase in total driving costs above the base case and produced a 20% reduction in daily trips, a 21.8% reduction in VMT and reductions of 23%, 19.6% and 28.5% in carbon dioxide, NOx and particulate matter, respectively.

A number of empirical studies have investigated the sensitivity of vehicle travel to various types of road tolls. These studies indicate a price elasticity of –0.1 to –0.4 for urban highways, meaning that a 100% increase in toll rates reduces vehicle use by anywhere from 10% to 40% (VTPI, 2002). Those elasticities are nearly three times higher than the general estimate by Johansson and Schipper (1997) of long-run elasticity for annual mean driving distance per car in relation to taxation other than fuel (between -0.04 and -0.12).

The research results now available from modelling studies suggests that it is possible to go beyond rough orders of magnitude in calculating environmental impacts from a given change in prices for specific transport routes.

# ENDNOTES

1.  The transport sector is defined for the purpose of this study as ground transport, with the emphasis on passenger transport. It does not attempt to cover international air transportation systems or international shipping transport, which do not receive as much attention in the literature on subsidies in the transport sector.

2.  Until recently, the OECD's Directorate for Agriculture, Food and Fisheries (OECD/AGR) referred to the PSE and CSE, respectively, as the producer and consumer *subsidy* equivalents. The term "subsidy" was changed to "support" mainly because it was felt not to be consistent with other economic terms that invoke an equivalency concept. However, some users of the concept outside OECD/AGR still use the original formulation.

3.  This study appears as a chapter in *The Effects of the FTAA Agreement on US Agriculture*, published by the ERS in 2002.

4.  One variant on the calculation of subsidy in terms of cost recovery for a set of irrigation systems covering a region or country includes only expenditures on the variable costs of the latest networks built (operations and maintenance as well as rehabilitation) but not the fixed costs (i.e. construction and depreciation costs).

5.  It is, in effect, the price that a monopolist would charge if it could price-discriminate.

6.  The possibility of constructing a PSE for the fisheries sector, as has been done for agricultural commodities and coal, was considered by the OECD Committee on Fisheries in the early 1990s but was rejected. It was argued that the technical obstacles to constructing PSEs for the fisheries sector would be too great and that the costs would outweigh the benefits because of the perishable and non-homogenous nature of fish products in the world market made it too difficult to establish reference prices by species for the purpose of calculating price supports (OECD, 1990; EC, 1990; OECD Committee on Fisheries, 1993a). Canada did not agree, however, that it was impractical to construct PSEs for fisheries subsidies, arguing that the value of price support through trade measures can be calculated for the entire fisheries sector of each country by dividing domestic sales by the sum of one plus the

tariff rate to provide an estimate of domestic sales that excludes the price increase provided by the tariff. The dollar value of the tariff measure can then be calculated by subtracting domestic sales excluding the tariff from actual domestic sales (Canada, 1990). By adding the total amounts of support from all three types of budgetary programs and valuing any loan guarantee and risk-reduction programs to the value of price support measures, it is possible to calculate a PSE for the entire sector.

7.      Australia has indicated in comments on an earlier draft of this paper that it will provide updated information on financial transfers to the forest industry for the November 2002 OECD workshop on subsidies.

8.      Several one-off studies of energy subsidies in the United States were also carried out in the early 1990s. The OECD (1997a), for example, published four studies that estimate subsidies broken down by programme; two of the studies had dramatically different high and low estimates.

# WEBSITES

Australia
www.budget.gov.au/papers/bp1/htm/bs6-01.htm

European Environmental Agency
http://reports.eea.eu.int/ENVISSUENo12/en/page025.html

Food and Agriculture Organisation
http://www.fao.org/waicent/faostat/agricult/meansprod-e.htm#prices

India, Department of Fertilisers:
http://www.fert.nic.in/usfert/dfg9899.htm#2401

International Energy Agency
http://www.iea.org/statist/index.htm

Japan
www.mof.go.jp/english/budget/pamphlet/cjfc_q06.htm

New Zealand
http://www.treasury.gov.nz/budget 2000

Organisation for Economic Co-operation and Development
http://www.oecd.org; http://www.sourceoecd.org

World Trade Organisation
http://www.wto.org/english/tratop_e/tpr_e/tpr_e.htm

Unification of accounts and marginal costs for transport efficiency
http://www.its.leeds.ac.uk/projects/unite/index.html

# REFERENCES

Ahmed, S. (1995), *Agriculture-Fertiliser Interface in Asia: Issues of Growth and Sustainability*, Science Publishers, Lebanon, N.H.

Amacher, G., R. Brazee, and M. Witvliet (2001), "Royalty Systems, Government Revenues, and Forest Condition: An Application from Malaysia", *Land Economics*, Vol. 77, No. 2, pp. 300-313.

Anderson, K. (1992), "Effects on the Environment and Welfare of Liberalizing World Trade: The Cases of Coal and Food", in K. Anderson and R. Blackhurst (eds.), *The Greening of World Trade Issues*, University of Michigan Press, Ann Arbor.

Anderson, K. and W.J. McKibbin (1997), *Reducing Coal Subsidies and Trade Barriers: Their Contribution to Greenhouse Gas Abatement*, Seminar Paper 97-07, Centre for International Economic Studies, University of Adelaide, Australia.

Anon. (n.d.), *Valuation of External Costs of Air Pollution*, Center for Research on Environmental and Health Impacts and Policy, Copenhagen.

Anon. (2000), *Report of the Quantitative Analysis Working Group to the FTAA Interagency Environment Group*, Office of the U.S. Trade Representative, Washington DC.

Asian Development Bank (2000), *Program Performance Audit Report on the Agricultural Program (Loan 1062-PAK[SF]) in Pakistan*, Asian Development Bank, Manila, http://peo.asiandevbank.org.

Aune, J.B. and R. Oygard (1999), *Guidelines for Integrated Plan Nutrient Management (IPNM in Smallholder Farming Systems*, Noragric Brief No. 3/98. http://www.nlh.no/noragric/research/Brief/brief3-98.htm.

Babu, S.C., B.T. Nivas and G.J. Traxler (1996), "Irrigation Development and Environmental Degradation in Developing Countries: A Dynamic Model of Investment Decisions and Policy Options", *Water Resources Management*, Vol. 10, pp. 129-205.

Barbier E.B., J.C. Burgess, J. Bishop and B. Aylward (1994), *The Economics of the Tropical Timber Trade*, Earthscan, London.

Barker, R., R.W. Herdt and B. Rose (1985), *The Rice Economy of Asia*, Resources for the Future, Washington, DC.

Bos, M.G. and W. Walters (1990), "Water Charges and Irrigation Efficiencies", *Irrigation and Drainage Systems*, Vol. 4, pp. 267-278.

Bowen, R.L. and R.A. Young (1985), "Financial and Economic Irrigation Net Benefit Functions for Egypt's Northern Delta", *Water Resources Research*, Vol. 21, No. 8, pp. 1321-1335.

Brouwer, F. (2002), *Effects of Agricultural Policies and Practices on the Environment: Review of Empirical Work in OECD Countries*, OECD, Paris.

Burfisher, M.E. (ed.) (2001), *Agricultural Policy Reform — the Road Ahead*, Agricultural Economics Report No. 802, U.S. Economic Research Service, Washington, DC.

Button, K. (1994), "Overview of Internalising the Social Costs of Transport", in *Internalising the Social Costs of Transport*, OECD/ECMT, Paris.

Cahill, C. and W. Legg (1989-90), "Estimation of Agricultural Assistance Using Producer and Consumer Subsidy Equivalents: Theory and Practice", *OECD Economic Studies*, Vol. 13 (Winter), pp. 13-43.

Cai, X., D.C. McKinney and M.W. Rosegrant (2001a), *Sustainability Analysis for Irrigation Water Management: Concepts, Methodology and Application to the Aral Sea Region*, International Food Policy Research Institute, Washington, DC.

Cai, X., C. Ringler and M.W. Rosegrant (2001b), *Does Efficient Water Management Matter? Physical and Economic Efficiency of Water Use in the River Basin*, EPTD Discussion Paper No. 72, International Food Policy Research Institute, Washington, DC.

Canada, Delegation to OECD Committee on Fisheries (1990), "Producer Subsidy Equivalent and the Fishing Industry: A Quantitative Example", paper presented to the 66th Session of the Committee for Fisheries, http://www.oecd.org/pdf/M00006000/M00006745.pdf.

CBD (Convention on Biodiversity) Executive Secretary (2002), *Assessing the Impact of Trade Liberalisation on the Conservation and Sustainable Use of Agricultural Biological Diversity*, Conferences of the Parties to the Convention on Biological Diversity, Sixth Meeting, 7-19 April, UNEP/CBD/COP/6/INF/2, The Hague.

CEC (Commission of the European Communities) (1991), Definition and Measurement of Trade Distortion for the Fishing Industry. AGR/FI/EG (91)6. Submitted to the 66th Session of the FAO Committee for Fisheries. 17 September.

CEC (1995), *Toward Fair and Efficient Pricing in Transport: Green Pape,* European Commission, Brussels.

CEC (2000), *Pricing Policies for Enhancing the Sustainability of Water Resources*, Communication from the Commission to the Council, the European Parliament and the Economic and Social Committee, COM(2000)477final, July 26, CEC, Brussels.

CEC Directorate-General for Transport (1998a), Proceedings of Seminar on Tolling Strategies and Experiences. EUROTOLL Project, No. RO-96-SC.101, CEC, Brussels.

CEC Directorate-General for Transport (1998b), Results of Case Studies. EUROTOLL Project on Toll Effects and Price Strategies, No. RO-96-SC.101, CEC, Brussels.

Clark, C.W., F.H. Clarke and G.R. Munro (1979), "The Optimal Exploitation of Renewable Resource Stocks: Problems of Irreversible Investment", *Econometrica*, Vol. 47, pp. 25-47.

Clark, C.W. and G.R. Munro (1965), "The Economics of Fishing and Modern Capital Theory: A Simplified Approach", *Journal of Environmental Economics and Management*, Vol. 2, pp. 92-106.

Clark, C.W. and G.R. Munro (1994), "Renewable Resources as Natural Capital: The Fishery", in A. Jansson, M. Hammer, C. Folke and R. Constanza, (eds.), *Investing in Natural Capital*, Island Press Washington, DC.

Constantino, L.F. (1990), *On the Efficiency of Indonesia's Sawmilling and Plymilling Industries*, Forestry Studies Field Document No. IV.5, LITF/INS/065/INS, Indonesian Ministry of Forestry and Food and Agriculture Organisation of the United Nations, Jakarta.

Contreras-Hermosilla, A. (2000), *The Underlying Causes of Forest Decline*, Occasional Paper No. 30, Center for International Forestry Research, Bogor, Indonesia.

Crosson, P. (1997), "Will Erosion Threaten Agricultural Productivity?", *Environment*, Vol. 398, No. 8, pp. 4-31.

Cummings, R.G. and V. Nercissiantz (1992), "The Use of Water Pricing as a Means of Enhancing Water Use Efficiency n Irrigation: Case Studies in Mexico and in The United States", *Natural Resources Journal*, Vol. 32, pp. 731-755.

Dauvergne, P. (1997), *Shadows in the Forest: Japan and the Politics of Timber in Southeast Asia*, MIT Press, Cambridge, Mass.

Day, B. (1998), "Who's Collecting the Rent? Taxation and Superprofits in the Forest Sector", Draft Paper, Centre for Social and Economic Research on the Global Environment, London.

Dean, J. (1995), "Export Bans, Environment and Developing Country Welfare", *Review of International Economics*, Vol. 3, No. 3, pp. 319-329.

De Jong, G.C. (1999), *Elasticity Handbook: Elasticities for Prototype Contexts*, Prepared for the European Commission Directorate-General for Transport, Contract No. R)-97-Sc-2305.

De Jong, G.C. and H. Gunn. (2001), "Recent Evidence on Car Cost and Time Elasticities of Travel Demand in Europe", *Journal of Transport Economics and Policy*, Vol. 35, pp. 137-160.

De Jong, G.C., P. Coppola and S. Gayda (1999), *Report on National Elasticities*, Prepared for the European Commission Directorate-General for Transport, Contract No. RO-97-SC.2035 (Costs of Private Road Travel and Their Effects on Demand, including Short and Long Term Elasticities), http://www.hcg.nl/projects/trace/trace1.htm.

Delucchi, M.A. (1997), *The Annualized Social Cost of Motor-Vehicle Use in the US, 1990-1991): Summary of Theory, Data, Methods, and Results*, University of California Transportation Center, University of California at Berkeley, Berkeley.

Delucchi, M.A. (2000a), "Environmental Externalities of Motor Vehicle Use in the U.S.", *Transportation Economics and Policy*, Vol. 34, pp. 135-68.

Delucchi, M.A. (2000b), "Should We Try to Get the Prices Right?" *Access*, Vol. 16 (Spring), pp. 14-21.

Denmark, Ministry of Environment and Energy, Environmental Protection Agency (1998), *Bekaempelsemidlernes I Egeskaber fra 1981-1985 frem til 1996* [Trends in Environmental Load of Agricultural Pesticides from the Reference Period 1981-85 to 1996] with English abstract, Ministry of Environment and Energy, Copenhagen.

Diao, X. and T. Roe (2000), "The Win-Win Effect of Joint Water Market and Trade Reform on Interest Groups in Irrigated Agriculture in Morocco", in A. Dinar (ed.), *The Political Economy of Water Pricing Reforms*, Oxford University Press, Oxford.

Dimaranan, B.V. and R.A. McDougal (2002), "Data Base Summary: Protection and Support", in Center for Global Trade Analysis, *Global Trade, Assistance, and Production: The GTAP 5 Data Base*, Purdue University, Indiana, http://www.gtap.agecon.purdue.edu/databases/v5/v5_doco.asp.

Dinar, A. (2000), "Political Economy of Water Pricing Reforms", in A. Dinar (ed.), *Political Economy of Water Pricing Reforms*, Oxford University Press, Oxford.

DRI/McGraw-Hill (1995), *Transportation Sector Subsidies: US Case Study*, Preliminary Draft Report to US EPA, for the OECD Environment Directorate.

DRI/McGraw-Hill (1997), "Effects of Phasing Out Coals Subsidies in OECD Countries", in OECD, *Reforming Energy and Transport Subsidies: Environmental and Economic Implications*, OECD, Paris.

EIA (United States Energy Information Administration) (1999), *Federal Financial Interventions and Subsidies in Energy Markets 1999: Primary Energy*, EIA, Washington, DC.

EIA (2000), *Federal Financial Interventions and Subsidies in Energy Markets 1999: Energy Transformation and End Use*, EIA, Washington, DC.

ECMT (European Conference of Ministers of Transport) (1998), *Efficient Transport for Europe: Policies for Internalisation of External Costs*, OECD, Paris.

ECMT (2000), *Efficient Transport Taxes & Charges*, OECD, Paris.

EPA (United States Environmental Protection Agency) (1999), *Indicators of the Environmental Impacts of Transportation*, EPA Office of Policy and Planning, Washington, DC.

European Environmental Agency (2000*)*, *Are We Moving in the Right Direction? Indicators on Transport and Environment Integration in the EU*, Environment Issues Series No. 12, Copenhagen.

Faeth, P. (1995), *Growing Green: Enhancing the Economic and Environmental Performance of US Agriculture*, World Resources Institute, Washington, DC.

Farah, J. (1994), *Pesticide Policies in Developing Countries: Do They Encourage Excessive Pesticide Use?*, Discussion Paper No. 238, World Bank, Washington, DC.

FADINAP (Fertiliser Advisory, Development and Information Network for Asia and the Pacific) (1996), *Fertiliser Policies and Subsidies in Developing Asia*, ESCAP, Bangkok.

Flaaten, O. and P. Wallis (2000), "Government Financial Transfers to Fishing Industries in OECD Countries", paper presented to the 10th Biennial Conference of the International Institute for Fisheries Economics and Trade, 10-14 July, Corvallis, Oregon, http://www.oecd.org/pdf/M00005000/M00005855.pdf.

FAO (Food and Agriculture Organisation of the United Nations) (1993), *Marine Fisheries and the Law of the Sea*, FAO Fisheries Circular No. 853, FAO, Rome.

FAO (1998), *Report of the FAO Technical Working Group on the Management of Fishing Capacity*, FAO, Rome.

FAO (2000), *Report of the Expert Consultation on Economic Incentives and Responsible Fisheries*, FAO Fisheries Report No. 638, FAO, Rome.

FAO (2001), *Report of the Ad Hoc Meeting of Intergovernmental Organisations on Work Programmes Related to Subsidies in Fisheries*. Fisheries Report No. 649, FAO, Rome.

Friedrich, F., P. Bickel, and W. Krewitt (1997), *External Costs of Transport in ExternE*, IER, University of Stuttgart, Stuttgart.

Gale, R., F. Gale and T. Green (1999), *Accounting for the Forests: A Methodological Critique of PriceWaterhouse's Report: The Forest Industry in British Columbia 1997*, The Sierra Club, Vancouver, BC.

Gallagher, K.F. Ackerman, and L. Ney (2002), *Economic Analysis in Environmental Reviews of Trade Agreements: Assessing the North American Experience*, Working Paper No. 02.01, Global Development and Environment Institute, Tufts University, Medford, MA.

Gardner, B.D. (1983), "Water Pricing and Rent Subsidy in California Agriculture", in Terry L. Anderson (ed.), *Water Rights: Scarce Resource Allocation, Bureaucracy and the Environment*, Ballinger, Cambridge, Mass.

Gates, J., D. Holland and E. Gudmundsson (1997), "Theory and Practice of Fishing Vessel Buy-back Programs", in *Subsidies and Depletion of World Fisheries*, World Wildlife Fund, Endangered Seas Campaign, Washington, DC.

Gillis, M. (1988a), "Indonesia: Public Policies, Resource Mismanagement and the Tropical Forest", in R. Repetto and M. Gillis (eds.), *Public Policies and the Misuse of Forest Resources*, Cambridge University Press, Cambridge.

Gillis, M. (1988b), "Malalysia Public Policies, Resource Management and the Tropical Forest", in R. Repetto and M. Gillis (eds.), *Public Policies and the Misuse of Forest Resources*, Cambridge University Press, Cambridge.

Gordon, H.S. (1954), "The Economic Theory of a Common-Property Resource: The Fishery", *Journal of Political Economy*, Vol. 62, pp. 124-142.

Gray, J.A. (1996), "Underpricing and Overexploitation of Tropical Rainforests: Forest Pricing Management, Conservation, and Preservation of Tropical Forests", *Journal of Sustainable Forestry*, Vol. 4, Nos. 1 and 2, pp. 75-97.

Gray, J.A. (1997), "Forest Revenue and Pricing Policies for Sustainable Forestry", Paper presented to the World Forestry Congress, Antalya, Turkey, 13-22 October 1997, http://www.fao.org/forestry/foda/wforcong/PUBLI/V4/T24E/2-16.HTM.

Greboval, D. (1999), "Assessing Excess Fishing Capacity at World-wide Level", in D. Greboval (ed.), *Managing Fishing Capacity: Selected Papers on Underlying Concepts and Issues*, FAO, Rome.

Grut, M., J.A. Gray and N. Egli (1991), *Forest Pricing and Concession Policies: Managing the High Forests of West and Central Africa*, World Bank Technical Paper No. 143, Africa Technical Department Series, World Bank, Washington, DC.

Hall, D. (2000), "Public Choice and Water Rate Design", in Ariel Dinar (ed.), *The Political Economy of Water Pricing Reforms*, Oxford University Press, Oxford.

van der Hamsvoort, C.P.C.M. (1994), *PSE as an Aggregate Measure of Support in the Uruguay Round*, Research Paper No. 122, Agricultural Economics Research Institute, The Hague.

Harley, M. (1996), "Use of the Producer Subsidy Equivalent as a Measure of Support to Agriculture in Transition Economies", *American Journal of Agricultural Economics*, Vol. 78, pp. 799-804.

Harden, B. (1996), *A River Lost: The Life and Death of the Columbia*, W W Norton & Co., New York.

Harold, C. and C.F. Runge (1993), "GATT and the Environment: Policy Research Needs", *American Journal of Agricultural Economics*, Vol. 75, pp. 789-793.

Haugland, T. (1995), "A Comment on the Paper by Ronald Steenblik and Panos Coroyannakis", *Energy Policy*, Vol. 23, pp. 555-556.

Hedley, D.D. and S.R. Tabor (1989), "Fertiliser in Indonesian Agriculture: The Subsidy Issue", *Agricultural Economics*, Vol. 3, pp. 49-68.

Heeringk, N.B.M., J.F.M. Helming, O.J. Kruik, A. Kuyenhoven, and H. Verbruggen (1993), *International Trade and Environment*, Wagingen Economic Studies, No. 30.

Holland, D.E., E. Gudmondsson and J. Gates (1999), "Do Fishing Vessel Buyback Programs Work?: A Survey of the Evidence", *Marine Policy*, Vol. 23, No. 1, pp. 47-69.

Hussein, R.A. and R.A. Young (1985), "Estimates of the Economic Value of Productivity of Irrigation Water in Pakistan from Far Survey", *Water Resources Bulletin*, Vol. 21, No. 6.

IEA (International Energy Agency) (1999), *Looking at Energy Subsidies: Getting the Prices Right*, OECD/IEA, Paris.

IEA (2000), *Coal Information 2000*, OECD/IEA, Paris.

IFPRI (International Food Policy Research Institute) (2001), "Crop Mix, Not Subsidies, Determines Fertiliser Use", *IFPRI Perspectives*, Vol. 23, Fourth Quarter, http://www.ifpri.cgiar.org/reports/01fall/falld.htm.

Isherwood, K.F. (1996), "Fertiliser Subsidy Policies in Regions Other than Asia and the Pacific", Paper for Conference on Fertiliser Subsidy and Price Policies in Developing Asia, 2-5 April, Bali.

Johannson, O. and L. Schipper (1997), "Measuring the Long-Run Fuel Demand for Cars", *Journal of Transport Economics and Policy*, Vol. 31, No. 3, pp. 277-292.

Johansson, R.C. (2000), *Pricing Irrigation Water: A Literature Survey*, Policy Research Working Paper No. 2449. Rural Development Department, World Bank, Washington, DC.

Johnston, R.A., C.J. Rodier, M. Choy, and J. Abraham (2000), *Air Quality Impacts of Regional Land Use Policies: Final Report for the Environmental Protection Agency*, Department of Environmental Science and Policy, University of California, Davis.

Jorgensen, H. and Jensen, C. (1999), "Overcapacity, Subsidies and Local Stability", in A. Hatcher and K. Robinson (eds.), *Overcapacity, Overcapitalisation in European Fisheries*, Centre for the Economics and Management of Aquatic Resources, University of Portsmouth, UK.

Kishor, N., M. Mani and L. Constantino (2001), *Economic and Environmental Benefits of Eliminating Log Export Bans—The Case of Costa Rica*, International Monetary Fund, Washington, DC.

Koplow, D. and A. Martin (1998), *Fueling Global Warming: Federal Subsidies to Oil in the United States*, Greenpeace, Washington, DC.

Lallana, C., W. Kriner, R. Estrela, S. Nixon, J. Leonard and J.M. Berland (2001), *Sustainable Water Use in Europe, Part 2: Demand Management*, Environmental Issue Report No. 19, European Environment Agency, Copenhagen.

Leppänen, J., M. Toropainen, and P. Vaisanen (2001), "Forestry Sector Financial Assistance in the Finnish Economy", in A. Ottitsch, I. Tikkanen and P. Riera (eds.), *Financial Instruments of Forest Policy: Proceedings of the Conference,*

*17-20 June, 2001*, European Forest Institute, METLA, IUFRO and the European Union, Rovaniemi, Finland.

Leppänen, J., Pajuoja, H. and Toppinen, A. (2001), "Effects of public support for forestry on timber supply", in B. Solberg (ed.), *Proceedings of the Biennial Meeting of the Scandinavian Society of Forest Economics*, Gausdal, Norway, April 2000, *Scandinavian Forest Economics*, Vol. 37, pp. 257-275.

Lindebo, E. (1999), *A Review of Fishing Capacity and Overcapacity*, Statejs Jordbrugs of Fiskeriokomiske Institut, Copenhagen.

Litman, T. (1999), *Socially Optimal Transport Prices and Markets: Principles, Strategies and Impacts*, Victoria Transport Policy Institute, Victoria, B.C.

Litman, T. (2001), *Transportation Cost Analysis: Techniques, Estimates and Implications*, Victoria Transport Policy Institute, Victoria, B.C., www.vtpi.org.

Lofgren, H. (1995), *The Cost of Managing with Less: Cutting Water Subsidies and Supplies in Egypt's Agriculture*, Trade and Macroeconomics Division Discussion Paper No. 7, International Food Policy Research Institute, Washington, DC.

LEEC (London Environmental Economics Centre) (1993), *The Economic Linkages between the International Trade in Tropical Timber and the Sustainable Management of Tropical Forests: Main Report to the International Tropical Timber Organisation*, LEEC, London.

Luyten, J.C. (1995), *Sustainable Food Production and Environment*, Report No. 37, Research Institute for Agrobiology and Soil Fertility, Delft, Netherlands.

McKibbin, W.J. and P.J. Wilcoxen (1996), *The Theoretical and Empirical Structure of the G-Cubed Model*, Brookings Discussion Paper in International Economics, www.brook.edu/views/papers/mckibbin/118.htm.

Marsden Jacobs Associates (2001), *Forestry and National Competition Policy*, Australian Conservation Foundation, Melbourne.

Mayeres, I., S. Proost, D. Vandercuyuseen, L. de Nocker, L. Int Panis, G. Wouters and B. de Borger (2001), *The External Costs of Transportation: Final Report*, Sustainable Mobility Programme, Federal Office for Scientific, Technical and Cultural Affairs, Prime Minster's Services, State of Belgium, Brussels.

Meyers, W.H. (1996), "Use of the Producer Subsidy Equivalent in Transition Economies: Discussion", *American Journal of Agricultural Economics*, Vol. 78, No. 3, pp. 805-807.

Mohd Shawahid, H.O., A.G. Awang Noor, N. Abdul Rahim, Y. Zulfiki and U. Razani (1997), *Economic Benefits of Watershed Protection and Trade off with Timber Production: A Case Study in Malaysia*, Economy and Environment Program for Southeast Asia, International Development Research Institute, Ottawa.

Montignoul, M. (1997), "France", in A. Dinar and A. Sumbramanian (eds.), *Water Pricing Experience: An International Perspective*, World Bank Technical Paper No. 386, World Bank, Washington, DC.

de Moor, A. (1997), *Subsidies and Sustainable Development: Key Issues and Reform Strategies*, Earth Council, San Jose, http://www.ecouncil.ac.cr/.

Munro, G.R. (1999), "The Economics of Overcapitalization and Fishery Resource Management: A Review", in A. Hatcher, and K. Robinson, (eds.), *Overcapacity, Overcapitalisation and Subsidies in European Fisheries*, Centre for the Economics and Management of Aquatic Resources, University of Portsmouth, UK.

Munro, G.R. and U.R. Sumaila (2001), "Subsidies and Their Potential Impact on the Management of the Ecosystems of the North Atlantic", in T. Pitcher, U.R. Sumaila and D. Pauly (eds.), *Fisheries Impacts on North Atlantic Ecosystems: Evaluationsand Policy Exploration*, University of British Columbia Fisheries Centre Research Report No. 9(5), Vancouver, B.C.

Nash, C. (2000), *Pricing European Transport Systems: Final Report*, Project No. ST 96-SC-172, Institute for Transport Studies, University of Leeds, Leeds, UK.

NIEIR (National Institute of Economic and Industry Research) (1996). *Subsidies to the Use of Natural Resources*, Commonwealth Department of the Environment Sport and Territories, Australia, http://www.ea.gov.au/pcd/economics/subsidies/subs11.html

Negri, D.H. and D.H. Brooks (1990), "Determinants of Irrigation Technology Choice", *Western Journal of Agricultural Economics*, Vol. 15, No. 2, pp. 213-223.

Nelson, F.J. (1997), *Measuring Domestic Support for U.S. Agriculture: How Producer Subsidy Equivalent was Used to Implement the Uruguay Round of GATT*, Market and Trade Economics Division, Economic Research Service, US Department of Agriculture, Washington, DC.

Nelthorpe, J., P. Machie and A. Bisnow (1998), *Measurement and Valuation of the Impact of Transport Initiatives,* Vol. I: Main Text, Contract ST-96-SC037: Socio-Economic and Spatial Impacts of Transport, Institute for Transport Studies, Leeds, UK.

Newberry, D.M. (1995), "Removing Coal Subsidies and the European Electricity Market", *Energy Policy*, Vol. 23, pp. 525-533.

Norway, Ministry of Agriculture (1999), "Environmental Effects of Trade Liberalisation in the Agricultural Sector", Paper submitted to the WTO Committee on Trade and Environment. 18-19 February, http://www.landbruk.dep.no/multifunctionality/html/environmental_effects_of_trade.html.

Nutzinger, H.G. (1994), "Economic Instruments for Environmental Protection in Agriculture", in J.B. Opschoor and R.K. Turner (eds.), *Economic Incentives and Environmental Policies: Principals and Practice*, Kluwer, Dordrecht.

Mahony, M., D. Geraghty and I. Humphreys (2000), "Distance and Time Based Road Pricing Trial in Dublin", *Transportation*, Vol. 27, pp. 269-283.

Oppenheimer, J. (2001), *In the Red: National Forest Logging Continues to Lose Millions*, Taxpayers for Common Sense, Washington, DC.

OECD (1990), "Various Methods for Measuring and Analysing Economic Assistance", Committee for Fisheries, http://www.oecd.org/pdf/M00006000/M00006739.pdf.

OECD (1993), "Inventory of Assistance Instruments in the Fishing Industry and Management Systems", Committee for Fisheries, http://www.oecd.org/pdf/M00006000/M00006772.pdf.

OECD (1995), *Review of Fisheries in OECD Countries*, OECD, Paris.

OECD (1997a), *Reforming Coal and Electricity Subsidies*, Working Paper No. 2. Annex I Expert Group on the United Nations Framework on Climate Change, OECD, Paris.

OECD (1997b), "Agri-Environmental Indicators: Stocktaking Report", Joint Working Party of the Committee for Agriculture and the Environment Policy Committee, OECD, Paris.

OECD (1998a), *Improving the Environment through Reducing Subsidies. Part II: Analysis and Overview of Studies,* OECD, Paris.

OECD (1998b), *The Environmental Effects of Reforming Agricultural Policies*, OECD, Paris.

OECD (1999a), *Improving the Environment Through Reducing Subsidies, Part III: Case Studies*, OECD, Paris.

OECD (1999b), *The Price of Water: Trends in OECD Countries*, OECD, Paris.

OECD (1999c), *Agricultural Water Pricing in OECD Countries*, OECD, Paris.

OECD (2000a), *Transition to Responsible Fisheries: Economics and Policy Implications*, OECD, Paris.

OECD (2000b), "Domestic and International Environmental Impacts of Agricultural Trade Liberalisation", Document No. COM/AGR/ENV(2000)75/FINAL, Directorate for Food, Agriculture and Fisheries and Environment Directorate, OECD, Paris.

OECD (2001a), *Environmental Indicators for Agriculture Vol. 3: Methods and Results*, OECD, Paris.

OECD (2001b), *Agricultural Policies in Emerging and Transition Economies: Special Focus on Non-tariff Measures*, OECD, Paris.

OECD (2001c), *Review of Fisheries in OECD Countries: Policies and Summary Statistics*, OECD, Paris.

OECD (2001d), *Environmental Effects of Liberalising Fossil Fuels Trade: Results from the OECD Green Model*, OECD, Paris.

Ottitsch, A., I. Tikkanen and P. Riera (eds.) (2001), *Financial Instruments of Forest Policy: Proceedings of the Conference, 17-20 June, 2001*, European Forest Institute, METLA, IUFRO and the European Union, Rovaniemi, Finland.

Paris, R. and I. Ruzicka (1991), *Barking Up the Wrong Tree: The Role of Rent Appropriation in Sustainable Tropical Forest Management*, Asian Development Bank Environment Office Occasional Paper No. 1, Bangkok.

Perry, C.J. (2001), *Charging for Irrigation Water: the Issues and Options, with a Case Study from Iran*, Research Report No. 52, International Water Management Institute, Colombo, Sri Lanka.

Porter, G. (1997), "Euro-African Fishing Agreements: Subsidising Overfishing in African Waters", in *Subsidies and Depletion of World Fisheries*, World Wildlife Fund, Endangered Seas Campaign, Washington, DC.

Porter, G. (1998a), *Estimating Capacity in the Global Fishing Fleet*, World Wildlife Fund, Washington, DC.

Porter, G. (1998b), *Too Much Fishing Fleet, Too Few Fish: A Proposal for Eliminating Global Fishing Overcapacity*, World Wildlife Fund, Washington, DC.

Porter, G. (1998c), *Fisheries Subsidies, Overfishing and Trade*, United Nations Environment Programme, Geneva.

Porter, G. (2002), *Fisheries Subsidies and Overfishing: Toward a Structured Discussion*, United Nations Environment Programme, Geneva.

Porter, G. (2002), "Agricultural Trade Liberalisation and Environmental Change in North America", Paper presented at the North American Commission for Environmental Cooperation Conference on Lessons of NAFTA, March.

PricewaterhouseCoopers (2000), *Study Into the Nature and Extent of Subsidies in the Fisheries Sector of APEC Members Economies*, Prepared for the Fisheries Working Group, APEC.

Proost, S., K. Vandender, B. DeBorder, C. Courcell, M. O'Mahony, R. Gibbons, Q. Heavey, R. Vicherman, J. Perison, E. Verhoef and J. Van der Bergh (1998), *TRENEN II STRAN: Final Report*, CEC DGII Transport Program Brussels:.

Rajkumar, A.S. (1996), *Energy Subsidies*, Draft Environment Department Working Paper, World Bank, Washington, DC.

Riedy, C. (2001), *Public Subsidies and Incentives to Fossil Fuel Production and Consumption in Australia*, Draft Paper, Institute for Sustainable Futures, , Australia, http://www.isf.uts.edu.au/publications/CR_2001.pdf.

Repetto, R. (1998), *The Forest for the Trees? Government Policies and Misuse of Forest Resources*, World Resources Institute, Washington, DC.

Ricci, A. and R. Friedrich (1999), *Calculating Transport Environmental Costs: Final Report of the Expert Advisors to the High Level Group on Infrastructure Charging (Working Group 2)*, 30 April.

Ringler, R., M.W. Rosegrant and M.S. Paisner (2000), *Irrigation and Water Resources in Latin America and the Caribbean: Challenges and Strategies*, EPTD Discussion Paper No. 64, International Food Policy Research Institute, Washington, DC.

Rodier, C.J., J.E. Abraham and R.A. Johnston (2001), "A Comparison of Highway and Travel Demand Management Alternatives Using an Integrated Land Use and Transportation Model in the Sacramento Region", unpublished paper, submitted to the Transportation Research Board.

Rørstad, P.K. (1999), "Effects of Nitrogen Levies and Permits — A Case Study for Norway", in *Economic Instruments for Nitrogen Control in European Agriculture*, CLM 409 – 1999, Utrecht, The Netherlands, pp. 107-124.

Rosegrant, M.W. (1997), *Water Resources in the Twenty-First Century: Challenges and Implications for Action. Food, Agriculture and the Environment*, Discussion Paper No. 20, International Food Policy Research Institute, Washington, DC.

Rosegrant, M. and R.S. Meinzen-Dick (1996), "Water Resources in the Asia-Pacific Region: Managing Scarcity", *Asian-Pacific Economic Literature*, Vol. 10, No. 2, pp. 32-53.

Roy, R. (1998), *Infrastructure Cost Recovery under Allocatively Efficient Pricing: UIC.CER Economic Expert Study*, International Union of Railways, Paris.

Ruijgrok, E. and F. Oosterhuis (1997), *Energy Subsidies in Western Europe: Final Report*, Report prepared for Greenpeace International, Institute for Environmental Studies, Vrije Universiteit, Amsterdam.

Runge, C.F. (1994), "The Environmental Effects of Trade in the Agricultural Sector" in *The Environmental Effects of Trade*, OECD, Paris.

Runge-Metzger, A. (1996), "Closing the Cycle: Obstacles to Efficient P. Management for Improved Global Food Security", in H. Tiessen (ed.), *Phosphorus in the Global Environment: Transfers, Cycles and Management*, Wiley, New York.

Ruzicka, I. (1979), "Rent Appropriation in Indonesian Logging: East Kalimantan, 1972/73-1976/77", *Bulletin of Indonesian Economic Studies*, Vol. 15, No. 2, pp. 25-51.

Ruzicka, I. and P. Moura Costa (1997), *Sustainable Forest Management: Allocation of Resources and Responsibilities*, Report for the British Overseas Development Agency.

Saleth, R.M. (1997), "India", in A. Dinar and A. Subramanian (eds.), *Water Pricing Experiences: An International Perspective*, World Bank, Washington, DC.

Sampath, R.K. (1992), "Issues in Irrigation Pricing in Developing Countries", *World Development*, Vol. 20, pp. 967-977.

Sansom, T., C. Nash, P. Mackie, J. Shires and P. Watkiss (2001), *Surface Transport Costs and Charges: Great Britain 1998*, Institute for Transport Studies, University of Leeds, Leeds, U.K.

Schorr, D. (1998), "Towards Rational Disciplines on Subsidies to the Fishery Sector; A Call for New International Rules and Mechanisms", in *The Footprint of Distant Water Fleets on World Fisheries*, World Wildlife Fund Washington, DC.

Schorr, D. (2001), "Evidence of Poor Transparency in Fishing Subsidy Programs", in *Fishing in the Dark: A Symposium on Access to Environmental Information and Government Accountability in Fishing Subsidy Programmes*. 28-29 November 2000, Brussels, World Wildlife Fund, Washington, DC, http://www.fishing-in-the-dark.org/docs/links.htm.

Schneider, K. (2002), *Global Coal Markets: Prospects to 2010*, Australian Bureau of Agricultural and Resource Economics, Canberra.

Schwindt, R. (1987), "The British Columbia Forest Sector: Pros and Cons of the Stumpage System", in T. Gunton and J. Richards (eds.), *Resource Rents and Public Policy in Western Canada*, Institute for Research on Public Policy, Halifax, Nova Scotia.

Sharp, B.M.H. (2001), "A Review of Published Estimates of Public Sector Subsidies to the Fishery Sector and their Impact on Trade in Fish and Fish Products", in *Papers Presented at the Expert Consultation on Economic Incentives and Responsible Fisheries,* Rome, 28 November -1 December 2000, Food and Agriculture Organisation of the United Nations, Rome.

Simula, M. (1999), *Trade and Environment Issues in Forest Production*, Environment Division, Inter-American Development Bank, Washington, DC.

Sizer, N. (2000), "Perverse Habits: The G8 and Subsidies that Harm Forests and Economies", *World Resources Institute Forest Notes*, http://www.wri.org/wri/.

Soejais, Z. (1999), "The Effect of Fertiliser Subsidy Withdrawal on Agricultural Development in Indonesia", paper presented at the International Fertiliser Association Conference for Asia and the Pacific, Kuala Lumpur, 14-17 November, http://www.pusri.co.id/Papers/Sujais-01.pdf.

Southgate, D. and M. Whitaker (1992), "Promoting Resources Degradation in Latin America: Tropical Deforestation, Soil Erosion and Coastal Ecosystem Disturbance in Ecuador", *Economic Development and Cultural Change*, Vol. 40, No. 4, pp. 787-807.

Spencer, G. and A. Subramanian (1997), "Water User Organisations and Irrigation Operation and Maintenance: Financial Aspects", in A. Dinar and A. Subramanian (eds.), *Water Pricing Experiences: An International Perspective*, World Bank, Washington, DC.

Squires, D., M. Alauddin and J. Kirkley (1994), "Individual Transferable Quota Markets and Investment Decisions in the Fixed Gear Sablefish Market", *Journal of Environmental Economics and Management*, Vol. 27, pp. 185-204.

Steen, I. (2000), "Industrial View on Agricultural Environmental Legislation", paper presented at the Second General Meeting of Nutrient Management Legislation in European Countries (NUMALEC), Thessaloniki, Greece, 18-21 May, http://soilman.rag.ac.be?~patricia/qm2C.pdf.

Steenblik, R. and P. Coroyannakis (1995), "Reform of Coal Policies in Western and Central Europe", *Energy Policy*, Vol. 23, No. 6, pp. 537-553.

Steenblik, R. and P. Wallis (2001), "Subsidies to marine capture fisheries: the international information gap", in *Fishing in the Dark: A Symposium on Access to Environmental Information and Government Accountability in Fishing Subsidy Programmes*. 28-29 November 2000, Brussels, World Wildlife Fund, Washington, DC, http://www.fishing-in-the-dark.org/docs/links.htm.

Stockle, C.O. (2002), "Environmental Impact of Irrigation: A Review", http://134121.74.163/wwrc/newsletter/fall2001/IrrImpact2.pdf.

Thiruchelvam, S. and S. Pathamarajah (1999), *An Economic Analysis of Salinity Problems in the Mahaweli River System H Irrigation Scheme in Sri Lanka*, Economics and Environment Program for Southeast Asia, International Development Research Center, Ottawa, http://www.eepsea.org/publications/researach1/ACF1D9.html.

Tiwari, D. (1998), *Determining Economic Value of Irrigation Water: Comparison of Willingness to Pay and Indirect Valuation Approaches as a Measure of Sustainable Resources Use*, CSERGE Paper GEC 98-05, The Centre for Social and Economic Research on the Global Environment, London.

Tiwari, D. and A. Dinar (n.d.), "Role and Use of Economic Incentives in Irrigated Agriculture", unpublished paper, World Bank, Washington, DC.

Toivonen, R., P. Maki and R. Enroth (1999), *European Union's Subsidies for Forestry and Agenda 2000*, Pellervo Economic Research Institute, Helsinki.

Toivonen, R. (2001), "European Union's Subsidies for Forestry and Prospective Changes by the Eastern Enlargment", paper prepared for the Conference on Financial Instruments of Forest Policy, 17-20 June, Rovaniemi, Finland.

Tsur, Y. (2000), "Water Regulation via Pricing: The Role of Implementation Costs and Asymmetric Information", in A. Dinar (ed.), *The Political Economy of Water Pricing Reforms*, Oxford University Press, Oxford.

Tsur, Y. and A. Dinar. (1997), "On the Relative Efficiency of Alternative Methods for Pricing Irrigation Water and their Implementation", *World Bank Economic Review*, Vol. 11, No. 2, pp. 243-262.

United Kingdom, Ministry of Agriculture, Fisheries and Food (1992), *Solving the Nitrate Problem, Progress on Research and Development*, MAFF, London.

United States Department of Commerce (1993), "Certain Softwood Lumber Products from Canada: Determination on Remand", 17 September.

United States Department of Transportation, Federal Highway Administration (1997), *1997 Federal Highway Cost Allocation Study, Final Report*, USDOT, Washington, DC.

United States Department of Transportation, Federal Highway Administration (2000), *Addendum to the Federal Highway Cost Allocation Study, Final Report*, USDOT, Washington, DC.

Varangis, P., C.A. Primo Braga and K. Takeuchi (1993), *Tropical Timber Trade Policies: What Impact Will Eco-Labeling Have?*, International Trade Division, World Bank, Washington, DC.

Varela-Ortega, C., J.J. Sumpsi, A. Carrido, M. Blanco, and E. YgIesias (1998), "Water Pricing Policies, Public Decision Making and Farmers' Response: Implications for Water Policy", *Agricultural Economics*, Vol. 19, pp. 193-202.

Vestergaard, N., D. Squires and J. Kirkley (1999), *Measuring Capacity and Capacity Utilization in Fisheries: The Case of the Danish Gill-net Fleet*, paper prepared for the FAO Technical Consultation on the Measurement of Fishing Capacity, Mexico.

Victoria Transport Policy Institute (VTPI) (2002), *On-line TDM Encyclopedia*, http://www.vtpi.org/tdm/tdm10.htm.

Vincent, J.R. (1990), "Rent Capture and the Feasibility of Tropical Forestry Management", *Land Economics*, Vol. 66, pp. 212-223.

Vincent, J.R. and C.S. Binkley (1992), "Forest-Based Industrialization: A Dynamic Perspecitve", in N.P. Sharma (ed.), *Managing the World's Forests*, Kendall/ Hunt, Dubuque, Iowa.

Vincent, J.R. and B. Casteneda (1997), *Economic Depreciation of Natural Resources in Asia and Implications for Net Savings and Long-Run Consumption*, CAER Project Paper No 614, Institute for International Development, Harvard University, Boston.

Vincent, J.R. and Y. Hadi (1993), "Malaysia.", in National Research Council, *Sustainable Agriculture and the Environment in the Humid Tropics*, National Academy Press, Washington, DC.

Vollebergh, H. (1999), "Energy Support Measures and their Environmental Effects: Decisive Parameters for Subsidy Removal", in *Improving the Environment through Reducing Subsidies, Part III, Case Studies*, OECD, Paris.

Vossiniotis, G. and D. Assimacopoulos (1999), "The Marginal Environmental Costs of Transport in Greece", *Global Nest: The International Journal*, Vol. 1, pp. 77-87.

WALHI [Indonesian Forum for the Environment] (1991), *Sustainability and Economic Rent in the Indonesian Forestry Sector*, WALHI, Jakarta.

Wallis, P. and O. Flaaten (2000), "Fisheries Management Costs: Concepts and Studies", paper presented to the 10th Biennial Conference of the International Institute for Fisheries Economics and Trade, 10-14 July, Corvallis, Oregon, http://www.oecd.org/pdf/M00005000/M00005848.pdf.

Warford, J.J., M. Munasinghe and W. Cruz (1997), *The Greening of Economic Policy Reform*, Vol. I: Principles, World Bank, Washington, DC.

World Bank (1993), *Indonesia: Sustaining Development*, World Bank, Washington, DC.

World Bank (1995), *Monitoring Environmental Progress: A Report on Work in Progress*, World Bank, Washington, DC.

World Bank (1997), *Expanding the Measure of Wealth: Indicators of Environmentally Sustainable Development*, World Bank, Washington, DC.

World Bank (2001), *World Development Report 2000/2001: Attacking Poverty*, Oxford University Press, Oxford.

WTO (World Trade Organisation) (2000), *Environmental Benefits of Removing Trade Restrictions and Distortions: The Fisheries Sector*, Note by the Secretariat, Committee on Trade and Environment WT/CTE/W/167, 6 October, Geneva.

WTO (2001), *Market Access: Unfinished Business — Post Uruguay Round Inventory*, Special Study No. 6, Geneva.

World Wildlife Fund (2001), *Hard Facts, Hidden Problems: A Review of Current Data on Fisheries Subsidies*, World Wildlife Fund, Washington, DC.

Young, C.E., M. Gehlar, F. Nelson, M.E. Burfisher and L. Mitchell (2001), "Options for Reducing the Aggregate Measurement of Support in OECD Countries", in M.E. Burfisher (ed.), *Agricultural Policy Reform — the Road Ahead*, Agricultural Economics Report No. 802, U.S. Economic Research Service, Washington, DC.

# SUBSIDY MEASUREMENT AND CLASSIFICATION: DEVELOPING A COMMON FRAMEWORK

*Ronald P. STEENBLIK*
*Trade Directorate, OECD*

## Introduction

Anybody wishing to analyse the broad effects of subsidies on the environment runs immediately into several problems. First, the only economy-wide data are those provided in systems of national accounts (which exist only for some countries), but the types of subsidies covered in these accounts are too narrow and relate only to gross transfers. The alternative, the various disparate compilations of subsidies to particular products, industries or sectors, which have typically been generated within distinct policy communities, are not readily comparable on account of differences in coverage and methods of calculation and classification. Moreover, because most subsidy data are compiled for other reasons, the categories into which they have been aggregated may not be appropriate for analysing their environmental effects. Finally, it may be difficult to map the subsidy data set onto information relating to environmental variables. The subsidy data may relate to a whole sector, for example, whereas the environmental unit of interest is product or technology specific.

Economists can cite totals of gross national income for different countries, or of other aggregates, with some assurance that the numbers are reasonably comparable. Not so with subsidy "totals". Within agriculture, at least, the total producer support estimate (PSE) for one commodity can be compared with a total PSE with another, owing to the fact that the estimates are produced by one and the same organisation. And economists working on subsidies to marine capture fisheries seem for the moment to have adopted the GFT (governmental financial transfers) as the default indicator. But for other products or industries, such as forestry and energy, no single dominant indicator or framework has emerged.

The reasons for these differences in subsidy accounts often have more to do with historical chance, and the prerogatives of the policy communities for which the work is done, than to intrinsic differences in the industries being analysed. This section seeks to establish to what extent the most important of the differences can be reconciled. Its basic premise is that the different approaches and frameworks *need* to be reconciled if progress is to be made in developing a more comprehensive and integrated view of the roles that subsidies play in influencing environmental outcomes, if not sustainable development in general. Such comprehensive and integrated views are needed not only to analyse the cumulative effects of subsidies, but also to reveal where they may be working at cross-purposes (Bagri, Blockhus and Vorhies, 1999).

This section is addressed in particular to the public finance economists, national accounts statisticians, and industry analysts responsible for producing and documenting subsidy accounts that serve as the primary sources of record. These include the people who produce published government budgets as well as those in academic institutions, intergovernmental organisations (IGOs) and non-governmental organisations (NGOs) who then rework the data for their own particular purposes.

It begins with a brief historical overview of how the concept of subsidy has evolved over time. As has oft been said, there is no universally accepted definition of a subsidy. That may be true, but there are certainly common themes that run through all the extant definitions. The important differences, in fact, relate more to the normative assumptions — which are not always made explicit — and the rules of thumb that practitioners use to set boundaries around their work, then to the exact wordings used to define subsidies. It would be pointless and fruitless to argue for a conceptually perfect definition. But practical criteria certainly matter, whatever definition is used it should be implementable with the available, or expected to become available, data, and consistent with the inferences that one wants to be able to draw from the assembled information (Bruce, 1990).

After reviewing some of the main conceptual issues, the question of the subsidy accounting framework is then addressed: that is to say, the classification system and aggregate indicators that one hopes to be able to produce from it. While most subsidy accounting frameworks have been developed for purposes other than environmental analysis, some are more useful for that purpose than others. This section addresses the question of what changes in, or additions to, the frameworks may be worthwhile making to better serve the needs of environmental analysts and policy makers, while still preserving the utility of the information for understanding the effects of subsidies on trade, competition, and welfare in general. Some suggestions of an institutional nature that the international community may wish to consider are proposed.

## The evolving concept of subsidy

Perhaps no testimonial has been more often quoted to summarise the frustration researchers feel whenever they try to pin down the concept of a subsidy than that of Hendrik S. Houthakker: "My own starting point was also an attempt to define subsidies. But in the course of doing so, I came to the conclusion that the concept of a subsidy is just too elusive" (JEC, 1972). Houthakker, writing three decades ago, could have just as well been describing the situation today.

Dissimilarities in the concept, and therefore in the formal definition of subsidies, arise largely from differences in the way the term has come to be used in everyday speech and by professionals working in separate economic and legal disciplines. Lexicographers trace the common usage of the word to the late Middle Ages, when the English Parliament granted funds to the king to supplement or replace customs duties and other taxes collected by royal prerogative. This practice eventually became the means by which the power of taxation was wrested from the king and vested in Parliament (Looney, 1999). The term has evolved since then to refer to any unrequited financial assistance including, in some dictionary definitions, that provided not only by a government but also by, for example, a philanthropic institution.

The tradition of accounting for government income and disbursements also has a long tradition, tracing back at least to Sir William Petty (1691), who is credited with being the first to prepare an account of national income (which he did as an intellectual exercise). Various independent and eventually government-sponsored efforts culminated in the development of an internationally agreed System of National Accounts (SNA), first published in 1968 (United Nations, 1968). In the revised 1993 edition of the SNA, subsidies are defined as "current unrequited payments that government units, including non-resident government units, make to enterprises on the basis of the levels of their production activities or the quantities or values of the goods or services which they produce, sell or import." This definition is among the most restrictive used by economists in that it covers only budgetary payments, and only those to producers — *i.e.* it excludes a myriad of other government interventions that give rise to transfers to or from producers or consumers.

The notion of a subsidy as, essentially, the inverse of a tax, assumes implicitly that the tax system is unbiased. But no sooner did governments start applying taxes as broad instruments of policy then they found ways to provide relief from those taxes to particular industries or sectors. In the 20$^{th}$ century, public-finance economists began to estimate what effects preferential tax treatment was having on government revenues, and to treat those foregone revenues as, effectively, subsidies. It did not take long for those attempting to measure monetary benefits to particular industries to combine these "tax expenditures" with normal budgetary expenditures in their calculations.[1] Other manipulations, by numerous practitioners (often those involved with the calculation of foreign subsidies, for the purpose of applying countervailing duties), led to further elaborations, augmenting the definition to include such support elements as the value of government loan guarantees or insurance liability, and government revenues foregone from not charging full costs for publicly owned assets.

Thus, through time, one can observe the gradual accretion of various types of transfers provided by governments and their agents, along with foregone revenues, to the more common notion of a subsidy as a direct government payment. Most of these additional elements are now reflected in the current definition of a subsidy given in the World Trade Organization (WTO) Agreement on Subsidies and Countervailing Measures (SCM Agreement). This agreement was signed at the end of the GATT-sponsored Uruguay Round of multilateral trade negotiations, and currently serves as the only internationally agreed definition of a subsidy (Box 1).[2]

The SCM Agreement is an instrument of international trade law, and must be understood in that context. Two exclusions from its definition stand out. The first is government-provided general infrastructure, which is not further defined in the Agreement. The term refers to government investments in such items as government-provided road networks, but not necessarily to a road built, for example, to service a remote mine or factory. The significance of this particular exclusion, and the more general distinction made between general and specific subsidies will be discussed below.

The second exclusion is price support, other than in the sense of Article XVI of the GATT 1994. Section A of this article refers to subsidies, "including any form of income or price support" and section B to export subsidies. Market-price support as the term is used by the OECD (transfers to producers provided through border protection) is thus not included, not because the GATT negotiators considered them unimportant, but because international trade law deals with tariffs and non-tariff barriers separately.

Economists as far back as Adam Smith and David Ricardo have recognised that border protection can be, and typically is, combined with subsidies to favour particular industries. The development of formal approaches to measuring the effects of border protection was helped greatly by the conceptualisation by Max Corden (1966 and 1971) of two aggregate indicators of protection: the nominal rate of protection (NRP) and the effective rate of protection (ERP).[3] The main difference between nominal and effective rates of protection (or of assistance) is that nominal rates refer to effects on gross returns to an activity, while effective rates refer to effects on the per-unit returns on an activity's value-adding factors.

---

**Box 1. Definition of a Subsidy in the Agreement
on Subsidies and Countervailing Measures**

1.1 For the purpose of this Agreement, a subsidy shall be deemed to exist if:

(a)(1) there is a financial contribution by a government or any public body within the territory of a Member (referred to in this Agreement as "government"), *i.e.* where:

(i) a government practice involves a direct transfer of funds (*e.g.* grants, loans, and equity infusion), potential direct transfers of funds or liabilities (*e.g.* loan guarantees);

(ii) government revenue that is otherwise due is foregone or not collected (*e.g.* fiscal incentives such as tax credits);[1]

(iii) a government provides goods or services other than general infrastructure, or purchases goods;

(iv) a government makes payments to a funding mechanism, or entrusts or directs a private body to carry out one or more of the type of functions illustrated in (i) to (iii) above which would normally be vested in the government and the practice, in no real sense, differs from practices normally followed by governments;

or

(a)(2) there is any form of income or price support in the sense of Article XVI of GATT 1994;

and

(b) a benefit is thereby conferred.

---

1. In accordance with the provisions of Article XVI of GATT 1994 (Note to Article XVI) and the provisions of Annexes I through III of this Agreement, the exemption of an exported product from duties or taxes borne by the like product when destined for domestic consumption, or the remission of such duties or taxes in amounts not in excess of those which have accrued, shall not be deemed to be a subsidy.

*Source*: World Trade Organisation (1999).

---

Soon after the ERP was first applied to Australia, once "infamous for having perhaps the highest manufacturing tariffs in the OECD" (Anderson, 2002), the concept was expanded so as to capture in principle all forms of governmental assistance to producers. This indicator, called the effective rate of assistance (ERA) measures the relative difference, expressed as a per cent, in the value added per unit of output with and without a given assistance structure. A companion indicator, the nominal rate of assistance (NRA) — also called the Price Adjustment Gap (PAG) after Miller (1986) — measures the percentage change in gross returns per unit of output relative to a (hypothetical) situation of no assistance.

Formally, the nominal rate of assistance to a product ($NRA_i$) can be expressed as: [4]

$$NRA_i = [(RD_i - PW_i)/PW_i] \times 100$$

where

$PW_i$ = undistorted (world) price for product $i$;

$RD_i$ = unit gross returns to producers for domestic output of product $i$.

The ERA for a product, $i$, can be expressed as:

$$ERA_i = \frac{AVA_i - UVA_i}{UVA_i} \times 100 = \frac{x_i - \sum_j a_{ij}(x_j)}{1 - \sum_j a_{ij}} \times 100 = \frac{NRA_i - AX_j}{1 - A} \times 100$$

where

$a_{ij}$ = an input-output coefficient (in the absence of support);

$A$ = set of input-output coefficients ($\sum a_{ij}$);

$AVA_i$ = assisted value added per unit of output;

$UVA_i$ = unassisted value added per unit of output;

$x_j$ = nominal rate of assistance (NRA) on the $j$th intermediate input;

$X_j$ = set of all net assistance on intermediate inputs, $x_j$.

The main limitations of the NRA and the ERA is that they require very detailed data — in the case of the ERA, input-output coefficients and information on input costs, both actual and undistorted. Accordingly, a truncated version of the NRA, the producer subsidy equivalent (PSE), was developed for use where such data were difficult to obtain. Timothy Josling (1973) was the first to apply the PSE, using it to measure support to agriculture. The PSE was then extended and refined by agricultural economists in the Directorate for Food, Agriculture and Fisheries of the OECD (1987) and the

Economic Research Service of the US Department of Agriculture (USDA/ERS, 1987). It has since been applied to measure subsidies to coal production (IEA, 1988; Steenblik and Wigley, 1990), and was eventually tried in the case of fisheries (OECD, 1993). Although not all institutionalised subsidy exercises use either the ERA or the PSE framework, there is now virtually universal agreement among economists that the concept of subsidy — or at least "support" or "assistance" — includes the effects of border protection.

These various composite measures of protection and support are measured against a counterfactual situation in which all else is equal except that the protection or support is absent; this is sometimes called the "neutral" or "positive" framework. It is also implicitly the baseline counterfactual used for most subsidy accounts. The notable exceptions can be found in current research related to transport, where some economists, cutting straight to the quick, have defined subsidies as deviations from a socially optimal ideal.

The paper by Nash *et al.* (2002), for example, identifies two totally different ways of applying that approach: the first compares total social costs with total revenues; the second considers the relationship between marginal social cost and price, and regards the failure of price to cover marginal social cost as a subsidy.[5] Among the "implicit" subsidies included in the former definition are those that arise from the failure to internalise externalities. These externalities typically relate to damage caused by air pollution, the (gross) costs to society of increases in $CO_2$ emissions, the economic consequences of noise pollution (such as impacts on human health and damages to buildings), and the costs of accidents not born by transport users.

Transport economists are not alone in using a normative definition of a subsidy. Since the early 1990s, an increasing number of environmental economists have mixed "conventional" subsidies with what they also refer to as "implicit" subsidies: damage to the environment and to human health caused by the activity in question. An early defence of this approach can be found in Reijnders (1990): "If one uses the wider meaning of the concept of subsidy, one may safely state that current activities are heavily subsidised by future generations of humans, third parties to the activity and other natural species." Analogously, some groups have also invoked the term "social subsidies" in reference to perceived benefits received by foreign competitors operating under labour standards that are lower than those applied to their own industries (Goode, 1998).[6]

In the first two of the above examples, uninternalised externalities generated by the economic activity in question are included in the definition of a subsidy. It is an approach that is intuitively appealing to economists accustomed to thinking in terms of Pigouvian (*i.e.* corrective) taxes and subsidies. For many reasons, however, it is extremely difficult to reconcile with the way public finance and other practitioners, not to mention non-professionals, understand the concept of a subsidy.

## Commonalties and differences in current approaches

Within the field of subsidy measurement two basic frameworks are applied: comprehensive accounting systems, as exemplified by the SNA, and sectoral subsidy accounts — *i.e.* accounts that relate to a specific product, industry or sector. For tracking government expenditure, national accounts can be very useful. Canada's SNA, for example, not only accounts for all government expenditure (including by provincial and municipal governments) but even provides details on payments to individual companies or institutions receiving CAD 100 000 or more in a given year (Public Works and Government Services Canada, 2002). For the purpose of analysing the effects of subsidies on economic performance, trade or the environment, however, the definition of a subsidy used for the purpose of national accounting is too narrow. This limitation is one major reason, in fact, behind the emergence of composite indicators of support, and of sectoral subsidy accounts. Also, national accounts report gross data and are not adjusted to take into account possible cost recovery through user charges or other recovery mechanisms (Schwartz and Clements, 1999). Nonetheless, the conceptual framework provided by the SNA provides a useful model, in as much as it embraces the entire (measured) economy and is internally consistent.

Sectoral subsidy accounts have their own sets of limitations, of course. A major one is that, by excluding non-specific subsidies, they leave out general subsidies that may affect the allocation of resources within an economy, in particular between different factors of production (land, capital and labour). A common example would be a non-targeted tax credit designed to encourage investment. The national accounts framework serves as a reminder that, ideally, the aggregation of all sectoral accounts should not leave any important gaps. This limitation, at least, can be addressed through the creation of a separate "unallocated" category of subsidies. A more important limitation is that the major subsidy measurement exercises, the ones that tend to inform policy debates, are prepared by different groups that, to varying degrees, cover different support measures and use different classification systems.[7] When arranged in chronological order (Table 1), the influence that established approaches have had on subsequent exercises can be readily observed. In addition, there would appear to be a close correlation between the adoption of a formal framework (as signalled by the use of aggregate indicators) and the establishment of a particular subsidy account series as the series of record.

## Table 1. Summary characteristics of selected international sectoral subsidy accounts

| Sector and Organisation[1] | Conti-nuity[2] | Production and/or Consumption | Market price support measured | Budgetary assistance measured | Tax expenditures measured? | Aggregate indicators |
|---|---|---|---|---|---|---|
| **Agriculture** | | | | | | |
| FAO | 2 | P | Y | some | N | PSE |
| OECD | A | P & C | Y | Y | Y | PSE, CSE, GSSE, TSE |
| **Coal** | | | | | | |
| IEA | A | P | Y | Y | Y | PSE |
| **Energy** | | | | | | |
| WRI | 1 | C | Y | N | N | — |
| World Bank | 2 | C | Y | N | N | — |
| IEA | 1 | C | Y | N | N | — |
| **Fisheries** | | | | | | |
| OECD | 3 | P&C | N | Y | Y | — |
| OECD | 1 | P | attempted | Y | Y | — |
| World Bank | 1 | P | N | Y | Y | — |
| APEC | 1 | P | Y | Y | Y | — |
| OECD | A | P | [Y] | Y | Y | GFT |
| **Forestry** | | | | | | |
| EFI | N/A | P | N | Y | Y | — |
| **Manufacturing Industry** | | | | | | |
| OECD | [A] | P | N | Y | Y | NCG |
| **Transport** | | | | | | |
| UNITE project | N/A | N/A | N/A | Y | Y | — |

1. See sources for corresponding references.
2. Key: A = annual basis; [A] = annual basis but discontinued; N/A = not yet determined; 1 = one-off study; 2 = original and one update; 3 = original and two updates.

*Sources*: **Agriculture**: Josling (1973); **FAO** (1975); OECD (2002); **Coal**: IEA (2001); **Energy**: Kosmo (1987), Larson and Shaw (1992), IEA (1999); **Fisheries**: OECD (1965, 1971 and 1980), OECD (1993), Milazzo (1998), PricewaterhouseCoopers (2000), OECD (2000b and 2001a); **Forestry**: Ottitsch (2001); **Manufacturing**: OECD (1998); **Transport**: Link *et al.* (2000).

These differences can be exaggerated, of course. In fact, the various sectoral accounts also share many common features. Most, for example, tend to apply a comprehensive view of government support measures; measure transfers (as opposed, for example, to changes in welfare) within a "neutral" framework; and generally exclude support that is not specific to the product, industry or sector. The significance of these starting points, basic assumptions and accounting conventions are discussed in greater detail in the Annex.

## Differences in coverage

With the exception of the various studies that have been undertaken to look at subsidies provided to energy consumers through artificially low energy prices, most sectoral subsidy accounts include budgetary payments. The main differences relate to whether separate accounts are provided for both production and consumption, and whether the accounts include estimates of market price support, tax expenditures and, where applicable, untaxed resource rent. In the following paragraphs, the significance of these omissions is noted both with respect to how they affect comparability among the accounts and whether they are likely to limit the usefulness of the accounts for the analysis of environmental effects.

### Production and consumption

The OECD's PSE/CSE database for agriculture measures support to both production and consumption. Most sectoral subsidy accounts focus only on production, however. The main exceptions have been in energy, where a series of international comparative studies have only measured subsidies to consumption. This tradition, concerned in particular with the stimulating effects of low prices on consumption of fuels that produce carbon dioxide or pollutants during combustion, was started by Kosmo (1987), further developed by Larson and Shaw (1992), and continued by the International Energy Agency (IEA, 1999).

Comparing subsidy totals that differ in terms of their coverage of production and consumption gives not only an incomplete picture but also a distorted one. Notwithstanding the limitations of assigning subsidies according to their initial incidence (see Annex), distortions can be introduced into either side of a market. Looking at only one side therefore can leave out information that may be important for analysing environmental effects. Accounting for subsidies to both production and consumption helps in understanding, for example, whether a low consumer price for petroleum products is being maintained through running down the productive capital of the domestic petroleum industry; subsidising domestic producers in order to cover their losses; or, in the case of a low-cost producer, preventing it (*e.g.* through export restrictions) from selling its product elsewhere and earning a higher price.

*Market price support*

Measuring the gap between the internationally traded price for a commodity, and the domestic prices received by producers for an identical commodity, has a venerable history in the trade literature, tracing back at least to the concept of the nominal rate of protection. This gap, when multiplied by the affected volume of production, yields an estimate of what in the terminology of the PSE framework is called market price support.

The measurement of market price support is inconsistently applied across the various sectoral subsidy accounts. It has been most-thoroughly explored and refined in the OECD's work on agricultural support. The IEA includes it in its subsidy accounts for coal. The IEA also applied a price-gap method for its one-off study of market transfers to consumers of fuels in non-OECD countries. Market price support has been incorporated, in principle, into the classification scheme currently used by the OECD's Fisheries Committee for governmental financial transfers to the fisheries sector. But it has not been included at all in the OECD's work on support to manufacturing industries (OECD, 1998; Lee, 2002). No internationally comparable accounts of subsidies to forestry have yet been prepared, but it is notable that the theoretical framework being used for the European Forest Institute's evaluation of "financial instruments of forest policy" (Ottitsch, 2002) seeks to measure several types of subsidy elements, including tax concessions, but not market-price support.

How important is the exclusion of market price support from some sectoral subsidy accounts? The answer to this question depends in part on the level of protection accorded the industry under examination. Recent analyses of tariff regimes following the Uruguay Round of multilateral trade negotiations show that both basic agricultural products and manufactured products using agricultural products as raw materials (*e.g.* prepared foods, hides and skins, textiles and clothing, footwear and headgear) still tend to be more heavily protected then, for example, mineral products or machinery, for which even bound tariffs tend to fall below 5% and 10%, respectively, in most OECD countries (OECD, 1999).

Admittedly, measuring market price support is easier for some products than others. It is more difficult for products that are harvested seasonally (like certain kinds of fish, and fruit), and for heterogeneous manufactured products, than for bulk commodities like crude oil or wheat. Nonetheless, practitioners working in sectors outside of energy and agriculture should not look only to what has been done in the context of subsidy accounting. As Bora *et al.* (2002) document, numerous techniques have been developed by trade economists for getting around the same kinds of problems. At the very least, applied tariffs could be used as a proxy for the price gap if no other method appears feasible.[8]

*Tax expenditures*

Perhaps no other subsidy element has been so controversial, and has so confounded attempts to measure it, than tax expenditures. The term itself betrays its origins in public finance economics, with its focus on government budgets. When a government provides a tax exemption, credit, deferral or other form of preferential tax treatment to an individual or group, its budget is affected in much the same way as if it had spent some of its own money. Alternative terms, which reflect more the perspective of the recipient, are "tax relief" and "tax concession".

The (opportunity) cost of tax expenditures can be measured in any one of several ways (OECD, 1996). The "revenue foregone"[9] method measures the amount by which revenues are reduced because of the tax provision. A related method, the "outlay equivalent" approach (used by the United States), measures what the cost would be to the government if it were to provide through direct spending the same monetary benefit as the tax expenditure. Both of these methods ignore possible changes in the behaviour of taxpayers in the absence of the tax expenditure. The "revenue gain" method (once used by France) attempts to account for such behavioural changes.

The majority of countries that measure tax expenditures seem to use the revenue-foregone method[10], hence it is the method that probably has been used to calculate most of the tax expenditure estimates included in the subsidy accounts reported by intergovernmental organisations, such as the OECD. Thus while most countries use the least-sophisticated of the three methods to calculate tax expenditures, in that regard at least the estimates are consistent. Inconsistencies arise nonetheless. A major problem is that great variation exists in the frequency with which countries report tax expenditures (from annually to sporadically), in the conventions used to distinguish specific from general tax relief, and in particular the provisions used to define a hypothetical benchmark tax system, or norm. As the OECD's 1996 study on tax expenditures observed, "clearly, the norm must reflect the structural stipulations of the tax system, but as the norm tends towards the actual system, so the list of tax concessions becomes shorter and the cost of expenditures reduces".

The result is that, while there is a generally held view among subsidy analysts (*e.g.* Pieters, 2003) that tax expenditures are under-reported, their incorporation into sectoral subsidy accounts has been piecemeal at best. Generally, the practice has been to include them in cases where the information is available, even if that means that those countries towards the more transparent end of the tax-expenditure-reporting spectrum tend to have their numbers counted as subsidies whereas other countries do not. In the OECD's 1998 report on public support to industry, over 50% of respondent countries claiming to provide tax-related investment incentives were not able to provide estimates of the net cost to government of these incentives. As the authors of the study remark, "If these gaps were filled, the amounts reported to date would increase considerably" (OECD, 1998). Yet, in spite of this under-reporting, tax relief accounted for almost two-thirds of total support to industry.

Problems of consistency among countries aside, is there any reason to suspect that tax relief plays a more important role for some products or sectors than others? This is difficult to answer because of the diverse forms of tax relief offered by multiple levels of government. At the local level, agriculture and forestry often benefit from preferential property taxes levied by local governments, at least in peri-urban areas, but so do manufacturing industries in some jurisdictions. Land devoted to roads and public parking facilities are typically not charged rent or taxes (Litman, 1999). At the national level, manufacturing industries often benefit from general investment incentives provided through the tax system (OECD, 1998). Tax relief offered to the energy sector varies considerably across both countries and fuels. The US Energy Information Administration (EIA, 1999a) estimated that 60% of the subsidies provided to production of primary energy in the United States in FY 1999 were in the form of tax expenditures, mainly relief on income tax. Almost half of the value of these tax expenditures benefited just one fuel (natural gas). Primary industries (*i.e.* agriculture, capture fishing, logging, and mineral extraction) in most countries benefit from tax relief on transport fuel used in boats and off-road vehicles.

*Subnational measures*

A sizeable share of subsidies is granted by sub-national governments. These are the government units, states in Australia, Mexico and the United

States, provinces in Canada, départements in France, Länder in Germany, prefectures in Japan, and so forth, as well as municipal governments everywhere, that administer smaller but often sizeable territories within sovereign countries. While sub-national units often have limited scope (either because of constitutional constraints or limited budgets) to subsidise industries, they do not universally practice *laissez faire*.

Coverage of measures provided by sub-national governments varies considerably among the sectoral subsidy accounts. The OECD's producer support estimates for agricultural generally include subsidies provided by sub-national governments; its estimates of government financial transfers to fisheries do not.[11] The OECD's (1998) study on support to the manufacturing industry noted that lack of information on sub-national programmes was one of the principal limitations of the study. Despite missing data at this level for several large OECD countries, programmes administered by sub-national governments were found to account for more than half of all assistance programmes and more than 25% of the funds spent. This share could very well increase in the future as central governments delegate spending responsibilities to lower levels, increasing the importance of monitoring sub-national subsidies. For example, the share of budgetary assistance provided to the German coal industry by Länder is expected to increase from 10% in 1997 to 22% in 2005 (IEA, 2001).

*Resource rents*

Some writers have suggested that un-taxed rent associated with the exploitation of publicly owned or managed resources should also be included in the subsidy accounting (*e.g.* Stone, 1997 and Milazzo, 1997). In particular, this argument relates to rent generated by governments not charging private individuals or enterprises for preferential access to a natural resource, such as a tuna fishery, a stand of pine trees or a gold deposit. A paper on environmental accounting in the Philippines (Virola *et al.*, 2000), for example, suggests that in that country taxes and other applicable fees are recovering only a small fraction of the rent being generated by fishing, forestry and mining. Rents can also arise in some service industries, such as when a government allocates specific electromagnetic frequencies (spectrum) to operators of telephone services.[12]

Resource rent accrues to an industry when its net revenues from exploiting the resource exceed the normal returns to factors of production. In the case of renewable resources, whether or not rents are generated depends in large part on the management regime. In open-access fisheries, for example, rents tend to become dissipated through expansion of effort (Clark, 1990). Management instruments that allow individuals to engage in profit-maximising behaviour, such as individual quotas (transferable and non-transferable) in fisheries, and exclusive area-use rights, may move fishing effort back to a level at which rents are again generated. These rents tend to become quickly capitalised into asset values, *e.g.* the price of quota, if they are not taxed away by the government. They are generally *not* taxed, except indirectly through income tax. It is fair to say, nonetheless, that the reluctance of governments to tax a portion of the resource rent that could potentially be earned from domestic fleets is a missed opportunity. (The opportunity is less often missed when foreign fleets are provided access; often *they* are charged a fee.) If the management instruments do not create conditions for the generation of resource rent to begin with, however, it is hard to justify counting that foregone revenue as support to the industry (Steenblik and Wallis, 2001).

The issue of how to treat resource rent in subsidy accounts merits more widespread investigation. Unrecovered resource rent is mainly relevant to primary industries, which use natural resources as factors of production, and then only where those resources are considered to be within the public domain. Examples from agriculture include the right to graze livestock on public land and to withdraw water from public reservoirs. Other cases may be less apparent. A head of water flowing through a geologically stable narrow canyon represents a tremendous potential resource. When a government-owned hydroelectric utility sells cheap electricity to local customers (even if it is covering its costs), but that kilowatt-hour price is below what it could charge for the same electricity were it to sell it instead to a neighbouring utility operating more-expensive coal-fired generating plants, are those local consumers receiving a subsidy?

## *Differences in classification systems*

Classification is the systematic arrangement of information into categories. Statisticians and analysts are naturally inclined to group subsidies into types, if only to explain succinctly what they have accounted for, and what they have not. Typologies of subsidies are typically organised around one or more of the following characteristics and dimensions:

- *target*: consumers or producers, outputs, inputs, value-adding factors (individual and collective);
- *instrument*: *e.g.* budgetary expenditure, tax expenditure, assumption of contingent liabilities,[13] market transfers, under-pricing of publicly owned or managed asset;
- *pathway of benefit*: direct, indirect, explicit, implicit; and
- *purpose*: *e.g.* regional development or energy conservation.

115

Subsidy accounts that have been designed with formal aggregate indicators of support in mind, such as the ERA or the PSE, tend to adopt a classification system arranged by the targeted recipient and stage of production or consumption, as these groupings are required to produce particular indicators of support. To the extent that these categories are comparable, they facilitate meaningful comparisons between countries and different sectors or products. Thus, one can observe in the IEA's accounts for coal, and the OECD's accounts for agricultural commodities, a significant shift in recent years from market-price support to other subsidy forms.

In many accounts, subsidy data are reported according to the instrument used to provide the support, either instead of by target or in addition to it. In both the OECD's subsidy PSE/CSE database for agriculture and its accounts for GFTs to marine fisheries, entries under the target categories often refer to the instrument used, but not always. In the OECD's accounts of public support to industry, subsidies are classified by both purpose and financing instrument; the latter category differentiates among grants, interest-rate subsidies, loans, loan-guarantees, injection of equity capital, tax concessions, and mixed instruments.

The European Forest Institute's data collection framework suggests a classification scheme for its correspondent researchers that differentiates between whether the measures are "direct" or "indirect" and, within these major headings, provides for the data to be organised by purpose (*e.g.* afforestation; fire-fighting and prevention).[14] The terms "direct" and "indirect" can be found in numerous other classification schemes, including those used by the OECD for fisheries, by the IEA for coal, and by the US Energy Information Administration for energy, among others. The terms themselves are of limited relevance to economic (or, by extension, environmental) impacts, though they can help explain the structure of the support system. Direct subsidies are generally those provided through targeted (cash-based) payments, loans or tax preferences (Bruce 1990; EIA, 1999b). Indirect subsidies are those that reach producers through market transactions, namely through higher prices for products or lower prices charged for input goods or services purchased from an upstream industry that is able to discount its prices because of the subsidies itself receives. An example of the latter would be a reduction in the cost of diesel fuel sold to fishing vessels as a result of subsidies to oil refiners.

The problem with using such terms as organising devices is that they have taken on widely different meanings. And no modifying adjective is more ambiguous than "implicit." To Bruce (1990), an implicit subsidy is a special category of input subsidy, generally provided in-kind by a government, at a price below its market value or insufficient to cover the costs of providing it.

Others have invested the adjective "implicit" with many more meanings (*e.g.* Legeida, 2002). Environmental economists in particular routinely speak of "implicit subsidies" when referring to the monetised value of (negative) environmental externalities generated by an activity.[15]

Finally, many sectoral subsidy accounts identify the professed purpose of the subsidy, and a few organise the data accordingly. While knowing the purpose of a programme may help in understanding the aim of government policy, it is an unreliable guide to real intent, much less hint at the subsidy's incentive effect. The euphemism "to improve the competitiveness of producers" has been invoked as a phrase to describe all manner of public policies, from retraining schemes to deficiency payments. Litman (1999) reminds us also that the widespread use of words like "improve", "enhance" and "upgrade" (instead of simply "change") in describing subsidy programmes benefiting particular sectors can indicate a policy bias in favour of one activity over others. For this reason, classification by purpose offers the least meaningful of the above typologies and, if it is the only typology used, renders different accounts non-comparable.

### *Differences in measurement and allocation methods*

Differences in classification systems explain only part of the reason why sectoral subsidy accounts are sometimes difficult to compare. Other variability is introduced through the methods used to calculate similar subsidy elements, in the practices used to decide which types of subsidies to include in the accounts and, when they are included, where to classify them. No systematic comparison has yet been made of these methods and practices, so it is only possible here to give a general impression.

As anybody involved in producing sectoral subsidy accounts will attest, calculating market price support involves as much art as it does science. The principle of the price gap is straightforward enough: ideally, it should involve a simple arithmetic comparison between a free-market reference price and the price received by producers (or consumers) for like products. Putting theory into practice, however, often requires considerable knowledge about the nature of the available price information and of the markets for the commodities being analysed. Often, adjustments have to be made to account for quality differences between domestically produced goods and those sold on world markets. Coal and other bulk commodities, for example, are processed to a higher grade before exporting, in order to avoid paying to transport unwanted impurities. Other adjustments are sometimes made to account for transport cost differentials, or to even out short-term fluctuations in exchange rates. The extent to which these various adjustments are made varies widely among different groups of subsidy accountants.

Another area in which practice differs considerably is the treatment of government expenditure related to infrastructure. Generally, the infrastructure in question serves one industry or sector predominantly, but not exclusively. Examples are irrigation infrastructure and harbour facilities in major fishing ports. Complicating matters, particular infrastructure projects may be self-financing overall, but involve significant cross-subsidies between groups of users (*e.g.* electricity rate-payers and irrigators served by the same combined hydroelectric/irrigation project). Some sectoral subsidy accounts simply count government investment in specific infrastructure as a subsidy to an input or value-adding factor. Others attempt to calculate optimal user charges for use of the infrastructure, and treat the difference between those charges and actual user charges as a subsidy. Perhaps because such a large proportion of government support to the sector is provided through infrastructure projects, analytical work in this area is farthest advanced in respect of irrigation and transport (Sur, Umali-Deininger and Dinar, 2002; Nash *et al.*, 2002).

Finally, practices relating to the treatment of missing data and the updating of previous years' provisional estimates can affect the degree to which the totals are over- or (more usually) under-estimated. The practice followed by the OECD's Directorate for Food, Agriculture and Fisheries when subsidy data relating to a particular programme (known to still be in operation) are not available for the current year is to use the expenditure data reported for the previous year, adjusted to account for inflation, where appropriate. Other accounts, however, appear to leave the entries for those programmes blank and produce totals on the basis of incomplete data. Most accounts are revised as new or more accurate data become available, but practices differ. Revisions are particularly important for what Schwartz and Clements (1999) refer to as "consignment subsidies" — *i.e.* loans provided in respect of projects (*e.g.* new energy technologies) that are only repayable should the project turn out eventually to generate a profit. The revenue-equivalent subsidy in this case may be only the value of subsidised credit if the project proves successful, but the full value of the loan (equivalent to a grant) if it does not.

**Building on common ground**

The preceding section examined some of the reasons why comparing, and especially aggregating, sectoral subsidy accounts prepared by different groups must be done with great caution and be accompanied by numerous caveats. The most important differences in the accounts relate to coverage, as these affect the total values. The ways in which the data are classified and reported tend to obscure these differences, which does nothing to discourage inappropriate comparisons being made. Developing a common reporting framework would at least address the latter problem. In addition, by highlighting the differences in coverage, a common framework would encourage researchers to fill in some of the missing information, even if those primarily responsible for the accounts do not themselves have the resources available to do so.

Do the elements for such a common framework already exist? If widespread usage is a germane criterion, then the answer is yes. Several of the sectoral subsidy accounts currently being prepared on a regular basis have been consciously guided by a formal conceptual framework — generally one designed to enable the calculation of a PSE (and sometimes a CSE) or an ERA. These frameworks in most cases were designed for reasons other than to analyse the effects of subsidies on production or consumption. That is not necessarily a bad thing. The relationship between subsidies and environmental outcomes is indirect, so there may not be any need to adopt a radically new classification scheme in order to ensure that the information can be employed by those who would measure environmental effects. Indeed, there are many obvious advantages to building on the existing frameworks, not least of which is the necessity to continue monitoring subsidies for the purpose of informing trade policy. However, there may be some additional information that needs also to be collected.

### *Adopting a common organising framework*

Organising subsidy data into categories that can be related to the production or consumption process itself — *i.e.* whether the subsidies are targeted to value-adding factors, intermediate inputs or outputs, or whether they seek to make up a deficit in revenues — enables useful aggregate indicators to be produced. More importantly, these categories are also those identified by economists as offering the greatest explanatory value for measuring the effects of subsidies on production (or consumption) and, as influenced by environmental or natural-resource management policies, on environmental outcomes.

The main purpose served by aggregating detailed data into composite indicators is to provide information that is more readily understandable than in detailed form. No single indicator can serve equally well all purposes (Anderson, 2002).[16] Many economists consider the effective rate of assistance (ERA), however, to be the best indicator of the incentive effects of protection and support on production. The ERA has one other virtue: the information required to construct an ERA, because it is the most comprehensive, can also be used to construct many other indicators, such as those related to the PSE.

Basically, in order to construct an ERA, one needs: *(i)* a reference (world) price; *(ii)* a domestic price received by producers; *(iii)* the volume of production; *(iv)* expenditure on intermediate inputs (or input-output coefficients); *(v)* the net effects of border measures, taxes and subsidies affecting the price of intermediate inputs; *(vi)* data on budgetary assistance to outputs; (vii) data on assistance to intermediate inputs; and (viii) data on assistance to value-adding factors (*i.e.* labour, land or other natural inputs; and capital). Calculation of a total PSE requires all of this information apart from *(iv)* expenditure on intermediate inputs, and *(v)* distortions affecting the prices of intermediate inputs.[17] The data requirements for these two items can be large, which is why the PSE has been used more often than the ERA in international subsidy accounting.

Most other sectoral subsidy accounts (an exception may be transport) could, with not too much rearrangement of the data, be fit into one of these frameworks. Table 2 shows how a generalised system of subsidy accounts might be constructed on the production side. (An analogous table for the consumption side could also be produced.) It is offered here merely as an illustrative example and is meant neither to be definitive nor comprehensive. The fact that it may not be feasible to fill in all the elements in all sectoral subsidy accounts should not itself be an argument against adopting a comprehensive model framework. The SNA, for example, can potentially accommodate a huge amount of information, but few countries report data in every area; but because its reporting conventions are common, statisticians from different countries can quickly tell what is in and what is missing.

Within the categories shown in the table, of course, one could add other sub-categories appropriate to the product or sector. For analysing environmental effects, for example, details on subsidies that encourage the use of natural resources (water, energy) in the production process are vital. It is also helpful to know not only whether subsidies are being targeted to capital equipment, but also to what kind of capital equipment they are being given.

## Table 2. Generalised framework for the production side of subsidy accounts

| | Variable | Units | Hypothetical example | |
|---|---|---|---|---|
| A | Production volume | tonnes | | 1 000 000 |
| B | Value of output | USDm | | 100 |
| C | Expenditure on intermediate inputs | USDm | | 45 |
| D | *Value added* | USDm | | 55 |
| E | Assistance to value-adding factors | USDm | | 5 |
| | 1. Land | USDm | 1 | |
| | 2. Labour | USDm | 2 | |
| | 3. Capital | USDm | 2 | |
| F | *Assisted value added = D + E* | USDm | | 60 |
| G | Assistance to outputs | USDm | | 15 |
| 1 | Market Price Support | USDm | 15 | |
| 2 | Payments based on outputs | USDm | 0 | |
| H | Assistance to intermediate inputs | USDm | | 4 |
| I | Miscellaneous payments | USDm | | 1 |
| J | Unassisted value added = F - (G + H + I) | USDm | | 40 |
| K | General Services | USDm | | |
| L | Producer Support Estimate (PSE) = E + G+ H + I | USDm | | 25 |
| M | Percentage PSE = (L / ([B - G2] + [L - G1]) * 100 | % | | 23 |
| N | Net subsidy equivalent = F - J | USDm | | 20 |
| O | Effective rate of assistance = (N / J) x 100 | % | | 50 |
| P | Nominal rate of assistance = (G / [B-G]) x 100 | % | | 18 |

*Source*: OECD Secretariat.

The classification scheme contained in Table 2 covers only one characteristic of subsidies: the targeted stage in production or consumption. Ideally, to the extent that other characteristics of support policies are meaningful, subsidy accounts should be multi-dimensional, containing information on both the mechanism by which support is provided (so that analysts can measure, for example, budgetary impacts) as well as the target.[18] Given the wide availability of relational database software, there is no reason (apart from the extra effort involved) why other dimensions could not be tracked as well. The critical design requirement is that the data be organised in such a way that aggregates under either category can be produced.

### Adding an extra dimension for policy parameters

In many sectors where government incentives are provided, controls are applied to limit inputs, production, harvesting of natural resources, or environmental damage or pollution. In theory, if these controls are effective, the production-stimulating effects of subsidies will be somewhat attenuated. Analysts must take such conditionality measures into account when measuring the environmental effects of subsidies to production (or consumption). They can themselves do the research necessary to identify which of the subsidies under examination are provided in combination with constraints on their production or pollution choices. Economies of scope in data-collection suggest that this value-adding activity can be done most efficiently at the stage when the subsidy accounts are compiled.[19]

Government officials themselves seem to have taken to the idea of adding this extra dimension to the classification of subsidies. In the late 1980s, in the context of its work on economic assistance, the OECD's Committee for Fisheries considered an analytical approach built around the construction of a two-dimensional "matrix" for assessing the effects of economic assistance programmes on the main variables governing the performance of the fishing industry (OECD, 1989). The "matrix approach" was revived again in 2001 by Hannesson (2001) in a report for the OECD, and by Porter (2002) in a report for the United Nations Environment Programme (UNEP). In both cases, subsidy types form one dimension, and the management regime (production constraints) or management conditions the other. Management conditions in Hannesson's matrix refer to whether or not the fishery is operating under an open-access, catch control or optimal management regime. In Porter's matrix, the effectiveness of monitoring and enforcement would also be taken into account. The matrix approach has not yet been applied empirically to fishery subsidies, as it requires information relating to individual fish stocks, whereas the currently available subsidy accounts relate only to national totals.

The essence of the matrix approach has also been applied in the classification scheme now used by the OECD to categorise subsidies to agriculture. In 1997 the OECD revamped its classification scheme in recognition of the importance of policies that seek to limit inputs or supplies. Thus, included among the various sub-categories of support to producers are payments that are conditional on limits being applied to output (*e.g.* dairy quotas), area or animal numbers (*e.g.* headage limits), or the volume of variable or fixed inputs used.

The potential applicability of the matrix approach to classifying subsidies could usefully be investigated for other sectors. With regard to forestry, for example, one could imagine including parameters relating to limits on contiguous areas that can be clear-cut. The main limitation of the approach is that it is difficult to nuance. That a subsidy is provided to dairy farmers, on the condition that they keep the density (cows per hectare) of their herds within specified limits, says nothing about whether or not the limits are within the carrying capacities of the pastures on which those contented cows graze.

### *Increasing the level of geographic detail*

Most data on subsidies are being collected at the national level, broken down further by industry or product. While such aggregate data are useful for the purposes of trade policy, or competition policy, they are less useful for correlating with changes in the environment. The possible exception is $CO_2$ emissions arising from the consumption of energy, for which national territories are currently the geographic unit of interest.

To assess specific environmental effects resulting from stimulated economic activity, information at a highly local or firm-level data are ideal. The rate, at which soil erodes, for example, is influenced by a constellation of factors specific to each farm. For any given level of fishing effort applied to a stock of a certain size and species, the difference between whether it is healthy or over-exploited depends in no small measure on the dynamics of its population, non-human predation, and a large host of local factors. Air pollution from traffic varies not only according to the level and mix of emissions but also the local topography, climate and prevailing winds.

Ideals, as a rule, are difficult to attain. Subsidy data tend to be reported at the national level because so many programmes are administered at that level. One may suspect that the central authorities monitor disbursements at a more disaggregated level, but obtaining such detailed information is quite another matter. Surely, the undisputed award for effort goes to the Washington, DC based Environmental Working Group (EWG), which showed that sometimes it is possible to obtain information down to the level of the individual recipient,[20] in their case owners of farmland. The EWG database relates only to direct, budgetary payments (*i.e.* cheques written to farmers), however, and has been built up from records of actual transactions.[21] Such records are amenable to computerised data processing — not so for tax expenditures benefiting individual recipients, computation of which requires knowledge of the recipients' overall tax status. Similarly, to estimate the values to individual consumers or producers of subsidies conferred through market transactions requires information on their purchases or sales. One can easily imagine the work that would be involved in trying to calculate the value of these subsidy elements on a farm-by-farm basis!

Unless a government is already providing comprehensive subsidy accounts down to a highly detailed geographical level, there may be a perfectly good reason why it should not: cost. For many environmental issues, resources that would otherwise be devoted to collecting and processing subsidy data could more profitably be used, for example, to conduct selected small-scale empirical studies on subsidies and their environmental effects.

**Possible next steps**

Subsidy accounting at the international level has made great strides over the past three decades, from being an activity largely focussed on agriculture to one that is being taken up by policy communities and experts working on energy, forestry, marine fisheries and manufacturing industries. The shift from being motivated mainly by an interest in measuring impacts of subsidies on trade, to analysing the effects of subsidies on a multitude of phenomena, but particularly environmental effects, is a more recent phenomenon. This intensifies the demands put on subsidy accounts and makes the need for achieving greater consistency among definitions, accounting methods and indicators all the more urgent.

Subsidy accounting would benefit greatly if an international consensus could be reached in these areas. It will be neither a quick nor an easy process. Attempts to achieve consensus on Systems of National Accounts (SNA) have been ongoing for almost half a century. Yet these efforts provide grounds for optimism, not pessimism. Suggested steps that could be followed to improve international subsidy accounting.

- Improve the publicly available documentation of subsidy data and methods. As long as the analyst's methods, sources and assumptions are well documented, other analysts can go back and revise the calculations or arrange them under different classification schemes. To date, such documentation has been highly variable. The OECD's Directorate for Food, Agriculture and Fisheries has for several years published CD-ROMs containing fairly detailed tables (though still at a level above primary data) of the transfers that make up its PSEs, CSEs and TSEs, as well as information on its calculations and data sources. And a User's Guide to its producer and consumer support estimate database is freely available on the web (OECD, 2001c; Portugal, 2002). The IEA also included information on its methods and sources when it published its first estimates of PSEs for coal (IEA, 1988), but that document has long been out of print.[22]

- Allow information to circulate more freely. That means making both the detailed results of subsidy measurement activities (and not just the summary indicators) and the documentation of the data and methods, easily and inexpensively available to others. The World Wide Web has already helped immensely in the dissemination of unpublished as well as published work, but better co-ordination of these sites, or the establishment of a centralised web site (as was created by the London Group of national income accountants and statisticians, for example[23]), would greatly reduce transaction costs and improve standardisation for practitioners new to the field.

- Ensure that peer reviews cross disciplines and institutions. At the international level, peer reviews of work on subsidies have mainly taken place within the institutions responsible for producing the subsidy accounts and between them and their governing bodies, which are usually specialist committees of government representatives from sectoral ministries. Occasionally, an independent researcher, such as Hamsvoort (1994) on the early agricultural PSE work, or a non-governmental organisation, like the World Wildlife Fund (2002) on fisheries subsidies, goes to the bother of critiquing what has already been published. Yet, until recently there has not been any serious attempt to encourage scrutiny of the sectoral accounts by a wider group of experts.

- Create a more-formal network of subsidy experts. The creation of the various "city groups" of experts working to improve the SNA could also be tried as a way of building a consensus on methodology. Such a network should involve participants representing a wide spectrum of professional backgrounds, viewpoints and countries.

Work on measuring subsidies at the international level can only be as good as the raw data collected and made publicly available by governments themselves. In this regard, parallel efforts need to be made to encourage greater transparency (and clarity) in budget documents, and greater consistency between developments at the international and national levels. Recent guidelines developed by the OECD's Working Party of Senior Budget Officials on best practices for budget transparency (OECD, 2001b), provide a useful reference tool in this regard.

**Concluding remarks**

At one time it may have been acceptable to consider the effects of subsidies from a partial perspective, sector-by-sector. Ministries of energy may not have been measuring subsidies in the same way as ministries of agriculture, but it hardly mattered: each knew where the trade-offs in their domains lay. Or, at least, that is how it seemed to them. The ideal of sustainable development, however, argues for taking a more integrated perspective, one that recognises the inter-connectedness of policies and their effects. Yet the fact that subsidy data currently differ so much from one sector to another confounds attempts to consider them across whole economies and allows vested interests to legitimately challenge each subsidy estimate as inconsistent with the others.

The paper has highlighted the fact that there remain important differences that may limit the degree to which economy-wide data on subsidies can be prepared from sectoral accounts. These disparities relate to coverage, systems of classification, and measurement methods. Determining where the significant differences exist is often hampered by inadequate documentation of assumptions, methods and data. Improvement of documentation would facilitate comparisons and peer review.

Adoption of a more common reporting framework, organised in such a way to enable aggregate indicators useful for monitoring to be produced, would help systematise the data collection and reporting. It is suggested that one structured around the data requirements for an Effective Rate of Assistance (ERA) could serve such a purpose, even if the available data do not currently permit the calculation of an ERA. Fitting the various sectoral accounts into a common framework would naturally expose differences in coverage more starkly, but that would be helpful, not harmful. It would also facilitate comparisons between sectoral subsidy accounts and National Accounts, if not the eventual integration of the two. Of course, consistency is a desirable end only to the extent that it does not inhibit necessary flexibility. We should not lose sight of the main value of subsidy accounts, which are the detailed data and metadata themselves.

126

Finally, in order to make sectoral subsidy accounts more useful for the analysis of environmental effects, some consideration may have to be given to the level of detail currently provided. Ensuring that subsidies to natural resources can be readily identified is vital. It would also be helpful to know whether subsidies are being targeted to particular types of capital equipment. Adding an extra policy dimension would make it easier for analysts to take into account any environmental-performance conditions placed on subsidy recipients. Whether it would be cost-effective to increase the level of geographic detail in the subsidy accounts is a judgement that has to be made taking into account the much greater effort involved in assigning subsidies to sub-national units and the value to be gained from correlating subsidies with localised environmental effects.

# NOTES

1.  One of the first was Schonfield (1969), who calculated "discriminatory subsidies and tax concessions" in Germany, based on data for 1961 derived from what he describes as "two elaborate calculations" by the [German] Ministry of Finance published in the *Bulletin* of July 1959 and the *Finanzbericht* of 1962.

2.  The separate WTO Agreement on Agriculture describes international disciplines applicable to basic agricultural products. In that agreement, the word "support" is invoked much more often than "subsidy" or "subsidies"; the latter terms are used sparingly, and primarily in reference to export subsidies, which are defined as "subsidies contingent upon export performance" [Article 1(e)].

3.  For a recent summary of these historical developments, see Anderson (2002).

4.  These equations are from Hamsvoort (1994).

5.  Economists at the Victoria Transport Policy Institute, in Canada, have reversed the hierarchy, making subsidies a subset of externalities. See Litman (1999).

6.  This is a particularly unfortunate use of the term, since it has long been used in Europe as a synonym for social-welfare payments and services.

7.  The notable exceptions are when single (usually government) institutions have produced sectoral accounts across their entire economies, such as Australia's Productivity Commission (and its antecedents) has been doing since the 1970s (*e.g,* Productivity Commission, 2001).

8.  The problem, of course, is that tariffs are not the only policy instruments that create a wedge between domestic prices and prices on world markets.

9.  The revenues here refer to those of the tax-collecting authority.

10. In a survey of national practice as of the mid-1990s, the OECD (1996: p. 14) reported that "All (fourteen of) the countries surveyed used the revenue-forgone method, probably as a result of the difficulty in computation and uncertainty in the results of estimates of behavioural responses."

11. The reasons have to do with resources available to do the work; they are not excluded by definition. Steenblik and Wallis (2001) have shown that some of this information can be obtained through budget statements available through the Internet.

12. One might immediately dismiss many services as uninteresting in terms of their effect on the environment. Yet any support that lowers the cost of mobile telephones — at least using current technology — can have tremendous consequences for waste disposal.

13. A contingent liability is an obligation taken on by a government, such as guaranteeing the repayment of a loan or playing the role of a re-insurer, for which the actual values paid out will depend on uncertain future events.

14. The EFI's list should be regarded as provisional and indicative. The final classification system that it uses for its final report may differ from this list.

15. For example, the British Government Panel on Sustainable Development's *Third Report* (1997) speaks of implicit subsidies as those "which occur where market pricing fails adequately to reflect external costs, for example those of pollution on the community as a whole."

16. The subsidy literature can give the impression that the primary objective of compiling subsidy data is to produce aggregate indicators of support. It is these indicators — the ERAs, the GFTs and the PSEs, or simply estimates of "total subsidies" — that tend to be reported in the press, and which are most familiar to those outside the policy communities from which they have sprung. Unfortunately, because of the emphasis put on aggregate indicators, misunderstandings about the level of detail that underlies them, and the degree to which their supporting frameworks can be adapted across different industries, arise all too often.

17. This statement is an oversimplification, of course. As Bora *et al.* (2002) observe, "PSEs relate assistance to the gross value of output (*i.e.* under existing intervention), whereas effective rates are based on free-trade levels of value added (or the free trade input-output ratio as shown in the formula)."

18. These two dimensions can of course be compressed into one (with one being a heading and the other a subheading).

19. That does not necessarily mean that classification of the second dimension can or should be done by the same people.

20. Any reference in this paragraph to subsidies provided to private individuals should not be interpreted as advocating disclosure of confidential data relating to

those individuals. On this matter, Principle 6 of the United Nations' Fundamental Principles of Official Statistics is quite categorical: "Individual data collected by statistical agencies for statistical comparison, whether they refer to natural or legal persons, are to be strictly confidential and used exclusively for statistical purposes."

21. There is not always a direct correlation between mailing addresses and farmed land. In their analysis of U.S. Department of Agriculture subsidy payments made between 1985 and 1995, the EWG identified over 74 000 recipients (accounting for 1.2% of the subsidies) whose cheques were sent to addresses within the city limits of New York City, Los Angeles, Chicago or one of the other top 50 US cities. See http://www.ewg.org/pub/home/Reports/Slickers/Contents.html

22. References are still being made to the original source document in the updated tables that now appear in the IEA's biennial report, *Coal Information*.

23. See http://www4.statcan.ca/citygrp/london/london.htm.

*Annex*

## Implications of standard assumptions and conventions
## used in subsidy accounting

### Using a "neutral" baseline counterfactual

Subsidies must be measured against some baseline, some counterfactual situation. Neil Bruce, in a conceptual study that he wrote for the OECD (Bruce, 1990), advised that subsidies should "be measured with respect to a counterfactual environment in which they do not exist, rather than as the deviation of the subsidy from its optimal value." In fact, many renderings of what that "counterfactual environment in which subsidies do not exist" might look like can be constructed.

When economists take numbers for budgetary grants and loans straight out of budget documents, and arrange them in subsidy accounts, the baseline they are implicitly using to define the subsidy is a very similar world but for one difference: the particular programme providing the subsidy does not exist. Yet the net value of such subsidies to the recipients will be to some extent offset by the increased taxes required to finance them. Adjusting subsidies to account for this effect would be impractical, and the results within the margin of error for the gross (unadjusted) subsidy. But, the theoretical point is worth bearing in mind when analysing the effects of large-scale changes in a country's pattern of taxing and spending.

Things become more complicated when one applies a price-gap method to measure transfers generated by border protection (*i.e.* market-price support), or the value to users of under-priced goods or services provided by governments. That is because one of the variables, the reference price, would likely adjust to a new equilibrium in the absence of the policy that gives rise to the price gap being measured. If the government of a country that was a large producer of wheat, for example, were suddenly to announce that henceforth all border protection and export subsidies would disappear, that countries' exports would drop in the short term and the reference price (usually the price at the border) would presumably rise.[1] The "true" value of the subsidy, to critics of the simple price-gap method to measuring market-price support, should thus be measured against the new equilibrium price, not the reference price prevailing

---

1. This outcome would be even more likely were all producing countries to reform their policies altogether and at once.

while the price-support policy is in place. A similar argument is often used by beneficiaries of government programs to justify "offsetting" subsidies or tariffs when overseas competitors are blamed for distorting prices in world markets.

This line of reasoning holds considerable appeal, and it cannot be faulted for being "wrong" in any economic sense. But, from a practical standpoint, it raises numerous problems. First, if it is to be followed for the calculation of market price support, then to be consistent it must also be followed in the calculation of direct payments to producers that are tied to a pre-determined target price — what in agricultural policy are referred to as "deficiency payments". That is to say, in that parallel universe in which no deficiency payments are given, production of the affected commodity would have been less, its price higher, and the required deficiency payment would have been smaller. Why stop there? Should we not also take into account the simultaneous effects of all the other subsidies that influence production and consumption levels?

Extending this logic to its inevitable end, one could make an argument for defining the counterfactual for subsidy measurement to be a world in which all subsidies, everywhere, are removed. Measuring subsidies against such a standard could only be done with the help of a computerised general equilibrium (CGE) model, and a very detailed one at that. As Bruce (1990) wrote, "Determining the hypothetical output and input prices in the economy in the absence of a government sector constitutes a major computational general equilibrium exercise, and even if this were done, the results would be subject to so much uncertainty that they would be of little interest." Granted, CGE models have advanced since 1990, but redefining subsidies as welfare effects, without going through the intermediate step of documenting the actual transfers, would sever any link they once had with observable data (such as expenditures published in budget documents) and render them irrelevant for monitoring budgetary impacts and other transfer-related purposes.

The introduction of normative criteria into the measurement of subsidies is problematic for several other reasons as well. One problem, which is particularly apropos to any discussion of potentially environmentally harmful subsidies, often manifests itself early on in the design of subsidy-measurement exercises: the temptation to divide subsidies into two broad categories: "good" and "bad". Increasingly, "bad" is defined in terms of the subsidy's presumed effect on the environment, or on the use of a natural resource, or even on sustainability. It should be readily apparent that if we are to objectively evaluate the effects of subsidies on the environment, the last thing we should want to do is define away the problem before we have even started!

Ironically, the fact that the word subsidy has more and more become a pejorative term has not helped those who would measure the thing. If a subsidy is, in popular parlance, something that is intrinsically undesirable, then, to a policy maker, characterising expenditure that provides net social gains as a subsidy risks exposing it to budgetary or other disciplines. As Shrank (2001) succinctly sums up the problem, "it leads to potentially endless diversionary discussions as to what kinds of activities are to be viewed as subsidies when the important thing is the role that these activities play in the economy." For the purposes of this paper, the word "subsidy" is regarded as a neutral term.

## Specificity

Basic to the concept of a subsidy is that it is a benefit conferred by a government that favours a particular activity or subset of its populace. Indeed, after satisfying demands for state-wide public goods, such as national defence, a major justification of government intervention in the economy is redistributive. On average, of course, we are all subsidised and taxed. Subsidies attract the interest of trade lawyers and economists, environmental and resource economists included, roughly in proportion to the degree that they favour particular groups, economic activities, or products. That is because the more they are "specific" to particular beneficiaries, the more they are presumed to be affecting resource allocation in the economy.

The word "specific" is placed between inverted commas in the previous sentence because it has a particular meaning in the context of international trade law. When a granting authority decides to send all eligible taxpayers a cheque for the same amount, as the US Government did in 2001 (for USD 300), few would call it a subsidy, much less specific. From the legal perspective of the WTO Agreement on Subsidies and Countervailing Measures, when a granting authority provides subsidies that "do not favour certain enterprises over others, and which are economic in nature and horizontal in application, such as number of employees or size of enterprise" then the subsidies are considered general (and therefore "non-actionable", *i.e.* not countervailable). However, when it explicitly limits access to a subsidy to an enterprise or industry, or groups thereof — whether explicitly in legislation, or through discretionary action, such a subsidy would be considered by most trade lawyers and economists as specific.

Much the same logic is used by subsidy practitioners when deciding which subsidies to ascribe to a particular industry or product, and which to regard as general. By definition, when subsidies are targeted to specific industries there is no ambiguity. And even when they are provided to several industries, rules of thumb can be applied to apportion the subsidies to different products. Thus, when confronted with a subsidy available to all livestock farmers, economists at the OECD will usually allocate the subsidy to different livestock products (beef, sheep meat, milk) based on either their relative values of production or livestock numbers, depending on the basis of the subsidy. In the rare cases where a subsidy is available to a significant proportion of producers in an economy, such rules of thumb become less useful, and deciding whether to attribute the subsidy to specific industries or products thus necessarily requires an element of judgement.

A slightly different notion of specificity intrudes occasionally into discussions on how to treat subsidies with significant positive spillover effects for the rest of the economy, *e.g.* subsidies to research and development. Generally, government support for primary research does not end up in detailed subsidy tables produced for agriculture, fisheries and energy. The reason for them not being there is that they are not specific, in the sense described above. However, some would argue that support to programmes that benefit the general public (or the state, if it has fiduciary responsibility over a public natural resource), more than the targeted industry, should not be counted as a subsidy. An example might be expenditure on protecting fisheries or public forests from illegal fishing or logging. This is a slippery slope: excluding government expenditure from a subsidy inventory because the public benefit exceeds the private can lead to all manner of claimed exemptions. Again, as long as it is understood that subsidy is a neutral term, the only meaning of specificity that can be made operational for subsidy measurement is one that avoids consideration of public goods spillovers.

## Incidence

Subsidy accounts usually make a distinction between production and consumption. The OECD's agricultural subsidy accounts mark the dividing line at the farm gate (*i.e.* at the point at which a commodity leaves the farm), for example. The subsidies are then entered in one or the other tables according to the target group. Nothing complicated about that, one would think.

Yet this distinction is what public finance economists refer to as an institutional one, not an economic one. In the real world, subsidies move around, split up and dissipate. In a buyers' market, for example, a producer subsidy can end up enriching consumers; in a sellers' market, a consumer subsidy can do the same for producers. Wolfson (1990) provides an excellent example of the latter. In the 1970s, following the first oil crisis, the Dutch government offered a subsidy to homeowners to encourage them to install thermopane (double-glazed) windows. The subsidy was offered at a time when producers of the windows were already operating at full capacity. What was intended as a consumer subsidy thus ended up as a windfall for producers.

In the example above, economic incidence differed from the initial-impact incidence because of poor timing. In many other cases, the onward shifting of benefits has more to do with policy design. Thus a subsidy that is paid out in proportion to the volume produced — *e.g.* a per-unit production premium — will not increase the income of the producer by the same amount as, say, a social welfare payment, because some of the money received will have to be spent on inputs used in producing the extra unit. This ratio between net income and the revenue-equivalent of a subsidy is what agricultural economists refer to its transfer efficiency.

Should subsidy accounts thus assign subsidies on the basis of their economic incidence, rather than their initial impact incidence? Generally, no. Attempting that for every subsidy would be an enormous undertaking, requiring knowledge of (ever-changing) short-run supply and demand elasticities. The results would also be subject to considerable imprecision. And it would blur the roles between subsidy accounting and analysis.

Subsidy practitioners do make exceptions to this rule, in situations wherein the initial recipient of a subsidy is merely acting as an agent for the government, and is obliged to pass on some or all of the subsidy to consumers or suppliers. An example would be when a government decides it would be quicker or less expensive to channel subsidies through an existing distribution network, as is often done to provide low-cost staple food to the urban poor. In this case, the subsidy, if it is indeed passed on as it is supposed to, should be treated as a consumer and not a producer subsidy.

## Drawing boundaries around the economic unit

Subsidies are usually ascribed to particular products or industries, and much less often to particular production technologies. In national accounts, the products and industries correspond to internationally agreed classification systems.[2] In the sectoral subsidy accounts, the boundaries are not always

---

2.    Respectively, the harmonised Classification of Products by Commodities (CPC) and the International Standard Industrial Classification (ISIC). Members of the North American Free Trade Agreement (NAFTA) use a slightly different system for industries, the North American Industry Classification System (NAICS).

specified, and are assumed to be self-evident. What is self-evident to some may not be to others, however.

Consider, for example, agriculture, the boundaries around which would seem to be pretty clear. Agriculture, or at least primary agriculture, is the sector that grows plants and animals for transformation into food, beverages, fibre, medicines and so forth. Yet there is some fuzziness around certain parts of the edges. The farming of fish resembles animal husbandry in many respects. Should it be included with agriculture, with fishing, or be treated apart? Should the growing of maize for ethanol count as agricultural production (*i.e.* defined by the productive activity) or as an energy activity (*i.e.* defined by the end product)?

The issue here is not one of correct or incorrect, but the importance of making clear to users of subsidy accounts where the boundaries lie. Without such information, those who would aggregate subsidies to different industries, sectors or products risk either leaving out a subsidy or double counting. In the second of the above examples, the situation could easily arise whereby a tax concession favouring ethanol over other motor fuels might be counted as a subsidy to maize (corn) consumption in the agricultural accounts, and as a subsidy to ethanol consumption in the energy accounts. Combining the agricultural accounts with the energy accounts without eliminating the double-counting would thus over-state the total of the two.

# REFERENCES

Anderson, Kym (2002), "Measuring Effects of Trade Policy Distortions: How Far Have We Come?" Discussion Paper No. 0209, Centre for International Economic Studies, University of Adelaide, Australia, http://www.adelaide.edu.au/CIES/0209.pdf

Bagri, Andrea, Jill Blockhus and Frank Vorhies (1999), "Perverse Subsidies and Biodiversity Loss", draft scoping paper for IUCN, The World Conservation Union and the Van Lennep Programme, Gland, Switzerland, http://www.biodiversityeconomics.org/pdf/topics-35-01.pdf

Bora, Bijit, Aki Kuwahara and Sam Laird (2002), "Quantification of Non-Tariff Measures", Policy Issues in International Trade and Commodities Study Series, No. 18, United Nations Conference on Trade and Development, Geneva, http://www.unctad.org/p166/modules/mod5/boralairdkuwa.pdf

British Government Panel on Sustainable Development (1997), *Third Report*, Sustainable Development Commission, London, http://www.sd-commission.gov.uk/panel-sd/panel3/6.htm

Bruce, Neil (1990), "Measuring Industrial Subsidies: Some Conceptual Issues", OECD Department of Economics and Statistics Working Papers, No. 75, OECD, Paris.

Clark, Colin W. (1990), *Mathematical Bio economics: The Optimal Management of Renewable Resources*, 2nd edition, John Wiley & Sons, New York.

Corden, W.M. (1966), "The Effective Protective Rate, the Uniform Tariff Equivalent and the Average Tariff', *Economic Record*, Vol. 42, pp. 200-16.

Corden, W.M. (1971), *The Theory of Protection*, Oxford University Press, Oxford, UK.

EIA (U.S. Energy Information Administration) (1999a), *Federal Financial Interventions and Subsidies in Energy Markets 1999: Primary Energy*, Report No. SR/OIAF/99-03, Washington, DC, http://www.eia.doe.gov/oiaf/servicerpt/subsidy/index.html

EIA (1999b), *Federal Financial Interventions and Subsidies in Energy Markets 1999: Energy Transformation and End Use*, Report No. SR/OIAF/99-03, Washington, DC, http://www.eia.doe.gov/oiaf/servicerpt/subsidy1/

FAO (Food and Agricultural Organization of the United Nations) (1975), *Agricultural Protection and Stabilisation Policies: A Framework of Measurement in the Context of Agricultural Adjustment*, FAO, Rome.

Goode, Walter (1998), *Dictionary of Trade Policy Terms*, 2nd edition, Centre for International Economic Studies, University of Adelaide, Adelaide, South Australia.

Hamsvoort, C.P.C.M. van der (1994), *PSE as an Agregate Measure of Support in the Uruguay Round*, Research Paper No. 122, Agricultural Economics Research Institute, The Hague.

Hannesson, Rögnvaldur (2001), "Effects of Liberalizing Trade in Fish, Fishing Services and Investment in Fishing Vessels", OECD Papers, Vol. 1, No. 1.

IEA (International Energy Agency) (1988), *Coal Prospects and Policies in IEA Countries*, OECD Publications, Paris.

IEA (International Energy Agency) (1999), "Looking at Energy Subsidies: Getting Energy Prices Right", *World Energy Outlook*, OECD/IEA, Paris.

IEA (2001), *Coal Information 2001*, OECD/IEA, Paris.

JEC (Joint Economic Committee of the Congress of the United States) (1972), *The Economics of Federal Subsidy Programs: A Compendium of Papers, Part 1 — General Study Papers*, U.S. Government Printing Office, Washington, DC.

Josling, Timothy E. (1973), "Agricultural Protection: Domestic Policy and International Trade", Supporting Study No. 9, Food and Agricultural Organization of the United Nations, Rome.

Koplow, Douglas and John Dernbach (2001), "Federal Fossil Fuel Subsidies and Greenhouse Gas Emissions: A Case Study of Increasing Transparency for Fiscal Policy", *Annual Review of Energy and Environment*, Vol. 26, pp. 361-89.

Koplow, Douglas and Aaron Martin (1998), *Fueling Global Warming: Federal Subsidies to Oil in the United States*, Greenpeace, Washington, DC, www.greenpeace.org/~climate/oil/fdsub .html.

Kosmo, Mark (1987), *Money to Burn? The High Costs of Energy Subsidies*, World Resources Institute, Washington, DC.

Larson, Bjorn and Anwar Shah (1992), "World Fossil Fuel Subsidies and Global Carbon Emissions", World Bank Policy Research Paper, WPS 1002, Washington, DC.

Lee, Frank (2002), "OECD Work on Defining and Measuring Subsidies in Industry", paper prepared for the OECD Workshop on Environmentally Harmful Subsidies, Paris, 7-8 November, www.oecd.org/agr/ehsw.

Legeida, Nina (2002), "Implicit Subsidies in Ukraine: Estimation, Developments and Policy Implications", Institute for Economic Research & Policy Consulting, Kyiv, Ukraine. Prepared for the United Nations Online Network in Public Administration and Finance, http://www.unpan.org/europe-casestudies.asp

Leppänen, Jussi, Mikko Toropainen and Päivi Väisänen (2002), "Forestry Sector Financial Assistance in the Finnish Economy", in A. Ottitsch, Ilpo Tikkanen and Pere Riera (eds.), *Financial Instruments of Forest Policy*, EFI Proceedings, No. 42, pp. 57-71.

Link, H, L. Stewart, M. Maibach, *et al.* (2000, October), *Accounts Approach*, UNITE (UNIfication of accounts and marginal costs for Transport Efficiency) Deliverable No. 2, ITS, University of Leeds, Leeds, UK.

Litman, Todd A. (1999), "Transportation Market Distortions: A Survey", Victoria Transport Policy Institute, Victoria, British Colombia, Canada. http://www.vtpi.org/distort.pdf

Looney, Robert (1999), "Subsidies", in R.J.B. Jones (ed.), *Routledge Encyclopedia of International Political Economy*, Routledge, London. http://web.nps.navy.mil/~relooney/Routledge_54.htm

Milazzo, Matteo J. (1998), *Subsidies in World Fisheries — A Re-examination*, World Bank Technical Paper No. 406 (Fisheries Series), World Bank, Washington, DC.

Miller, Geoff (1986), *The Political Economy of International Agricultural Policy Reform*, Australian Government Publishing Service, Canberra.

Nash, Chris, Peter Bickel, Rainer Friedrich, Heike Link and Louise Stewart (2002), "The Environmental Impact of Transport Subsidies", paper prepared for the OECD Workshop on Environmentally Harmful Subsidies, Paris, 7-8 November, www.oecd.org/agr/ehsw.

OECD (Organisation for Economic Co-operation and Development) (1965, 1971 and 1980), *Financial Support to the Fishing Industry*, OECD, Paris.

OECD (1987), *National Policies and Agricultural Trade*, OECD, Paris.

OECD (1989), "Economic Assistance to the Fishing Industry", Committee for Fisheries, http://www.oecd.org/pdf/M00006000/M00006733.pdf.

OECD (1993), "The Cod Study", Committee for Fisheries, http://www.oecd.org/pdf/M00006000/M00006742.pdf, 3 November 1993.

OECD (1996), *Tax Expenditures: Recent Experiences*, OECD, Paris.

OECD (1998), *Spotlight on Public Support to Industry*, OECD, Paris.

OECD (1999), *Post-Uruguay Round Tariff Regimes: Achievements and Outlook*, OECD, Paris.

OECD (2000a), *Review of Fisheries in OECD Countries,* Vol. 1 and 2, OECD, Paris.

OECD (2000b), *Transition to Responsible Fisheries: Economic and Policy Implications*, OECD, Paris.

OECD (2001a), "Environmental Effects of Liberalising Fossil Fuels Trade: Results from the OECD Green Model", OECD Document No. COM/TD/ENV(2000)38/FINAL, Paris, http://www.olis.oecd.org/olis/2000doc.nsf/c5ce8ffa41835d64c125685d005300b0/c125692700623b74c1256acb002e6b09/$FILE/JT00112751.DOC

OECD (2001b), *OECD Best Practices for Budget Transparency*, OECD, Paris. http://www.oecd.org/pdf/M00021000/M00021145.pdf

OECD (2001c), *Producer and Consumer Support Estimates: OECD Database —
User's Guide*, OECD Publications, Paris. Available at
http://www.oecd.org/pdf/M00022000/M00022612.pdf

OECD (2002), *Agricultural Policies in OECD Countries: Monitoring and Evaluation*,
OECD, Paris.

Ottitsch, Andreas (2002), "A Theoretical Framework for the Evaluation of Financial
Instruments of Forest Policy", in A. Ottitsch, Ilpo Tikkanen and Pere Riera
(eds.), *Financial Instruments of Forest Policy*, EFI Proceedings, No. 42, pp. 29-
42.

Petty, Sir William (1691), "Verburn Saplenti, or an Account of the Wealth and
Expences of England, and the Method of raising Taxes in the most Equal
Manner", written in 1665, printed in 1691 in N. Tate (ed.), *The Political
Anatomy of Ireland*.

Pieters, Jan (2003), "What Makes a Subsidy Environmentally Harmful: Developing a
Checklist Based on the Conditionality of Subsidies", paper prepared for the
OECD Workshop on Environmentally Harmful Subsidies, Paris, 7-8 November,
published in this volume.

Porter, Gareth (2003), "Subsidies and the Environment: An Overview of the State of
Knowledge", paper prepared for the OECD Workshop on Environmentally
Harmful Subsidies, Paris, 7-8 November, published in this volume.

Portugal, Luis (2002), "Methodology for the Measurement of Support and Use in Policy
Evaluation", OECD Directorate for Food, Agriculture and Fisheries, Paris,
http://www.oecd.org/pdf/M00031000/M00031750.pdf

PricewaterhouseCoopers (2000), *Study Into the Nature and Extent of Subsidies in the
Fisheries Sector of APEC Members Economies*, APEC Publication No. APEC
#00-FS-01.1, APEC Secretariat, Singapore, http://www.apecsec.org.sg/
download/fwg/fish_subsidy.exe

Productivity Commission (2001), *Trade & Assistance Review 2000-2001*, Annual
Report Series, AusInfo, Canberra, http://www.pc.gov.au/research/annrpt/
tar0001/index.html.

Public Works and Government Services Canada (2002), *2001-2002 Public Accounts Of
Canada: Transfer Payments*, Government of Canada Publications, Ottawa,
http://www.pwgsc.gc.ca/recgen/text/pub-acc-e.html.

Reijnders, Lucus (1990), "Subsidies and the Environment" in Ronald Gerritse (ed.),
*Producer Subsidies*, Pinter Publishers, London and New York, pp. 111-121.

Schrank, William E. (2001), "Subsidies for Fisheries: A Review of Concepts", in
*Papers Presented at the Expert Consultation on Economic Incentives and
Responsible Fisheries, Rome, 28 November – 1 December 2000*, FAO Fisheries
Report No. 638, Supplement, Food and Agricultural Organization of the United
Nations, Rome, pp. 11-39.

Schonfield, Andrew (1969), *Modern Capitalism: The Changing Balance of Public and Private Power*, Oxford University Press, London and New York.

Schwartz, Gerd and Benedict Clements (1999), "Government Subsidies", *Journal of Economic Surveys*, Vol. 13, No. 2, pp. 119-148.

Steenblik, R. and P. Wallis (2001), "Subsidies to Marine Capture Fisheries: The International Information Gap", in *Fishing in the Dark, A Symposium on Access to Environmental Information and Government Accountability in Fishing Subsidy Programmes*, World Wildlife Fund, Endangered Seas Campaign, Washington, DC, pp. 17-39.

Steenblik, Ronald P. and Kenneth J. Wigley (1990), "Coal Policies and Trade Barriers", *Energy Policy*, Vol. 18, No. 5, May, pp. 351-367.

Stone, Christopher (1997), "Too Many Fishing Boats, Too Few Fish: Can Trade Laws Trim Subsidies and Restore the Balance in Global Fisheries?", *Environmental Law Quarterly*, Vol. 24, No. 3, pp. 504-44.

Sur, Mona, Dina Umali-Deininger and Ariel Dinar (2002), "Water-related Subsidies in Agriculture: Environmental and Equity Consequences", paper prepared for the OECD Workshop on Environmentally Harmful Subsidies, Paris, 7-8 November, www.oecd.org/agr/ehsw.

United Nations (1968), *A System of National Accounts (SNA)*, United Nations, New York.

USDA/ERS (U.S. Department of Agriculture, Economic Research Service) (1987), *Government Intervention in Agriculture: Measurement, Evaluation and Implications for Trade Negotiations*, Foreign Agricultural Economic Report No. 229, Washington, DC.

Virola, Romulo A., Sylvia M. De Perio and Eduardo T. Angeles (2000), "Environmental Accounting in the Philippines", paper presented during the Users' Forum on Environmental Accounting, Makati City, 29 June.

Wolfson, Dirk (1990), "Towards a Theory of Subsidization", in Ronald Gerritse (ed.), *Producer Subsidies*, Pinter Publishers, London and New York, pp. 1-19.

World Trade Organisation (1999), *The results of the Uruguay Round of Multilateral Trade Negotiations: The Legal Texts*, Geneva.

World Wildlife Fund (2001), *Hard Facts, Hidden Problems: A Review of Current Data on Fishing Subsidies*, WWF Technical Paper, Gland, Switzerland, http://www.worldwildlife.org/oceans/hard_facts.pdf.

# WHEN REMOVING SUBSIDIES BENEFITS THE ENVIRONMENT: DEVELOPING A CHECKLIST BASED ON THE CONDITIONALITY OF SUBSIDIES

*Jan Pieters*
*Ministry of Housing, Spatial Planning and Environment*
*The Netherlands*

## Introduction

### Context

Since the early nineties, reforming or removing[1] subsidies in order to improve the environment have been high on the international political agenda. Many studies on the environmental effects of subsidies have been published (for an overview, see Gareth Porter, 2003). Between 1992-1997, the OECD embarked on a comprehensive project on the environmental implications of energy and transport subsidies, resulting in numerous case studies and a final summary report, *Reforming Energy and Transport Subsidies: Environmental and Economic implications* (OECD, 1997). These studies, which applied various elaborate definitions of subsidies, revealed a complex picture and led to the conclusion that previous studies may have overestimated the environmental benefits of their removal. Environmental effects of subsidies appeared to be rather sensitive to circumstances as well as assumptions on which the quantitative analyses were based.

In 1995, G7 Ministers requested the OECD to carry out a study on the costs and benefits of eliminating or reforming subsidies and tax disincentives to sound environmental practices in various sectors. This project resulted in a major report, *Improving the Environment through Reducing Subsidies* (OECD, 1998, 1999). This project resulted in, among other things, a rudimentary and not-so-easy-to-apply "quick scan"(OECD, 1998 Part II) that would allow for selecting those subsidies that were more likely than others to have adverse environmental effects, while having small effects on their stated objectives (notably, employment and income). This "quick scan" more or less automatically emerged when trying to systemise the then available evidence and looking for common factors that have a decisive impact on the environmental effects of subsidy removal. The present study can be seen as an elaboration of this "quick scan", while being confined to environmental effects only.

## Why develop a checklist

Developing a checklist may serve two purposes:

- It could help to focus the attention to those conditions under which subsidy removal could indeed have significant beneficial environmental effects. Identifying those conditions is the prime purpose of this exercise.

- When eventually developed successfully, governments could apply the checklist to any set of subsidies that they are considering for removal (on whatever grounds)[2] and (provisionally) rank them according to their environmental effects (when removed). Since subsidies are difficult to remove, focusing on the removal of subsidies that have a significant impact on the environment seems important.

It should be noted that, given this envisaged use of the checklist, this paper and its underlying reasoning does not give additional guidance on how to define subsidies. Governments have already a list of subsidies according to whatever definition(s) they consider to be appropriate. Also the checklist will not contain items referring to the dose response relations that determine the nature and magnitude of the environmental effects of rates of exploitation and pollution, as well as items concerning the emissions and resource requirements ("environmental profiles") of industries. It is assumed that governments already have that information. The checklist merely lists important questions that must be answered to decide whether subsidy removal is likely to remedy adverse environmental effects, without creating other negative environmental impacts.

A checklist that is applicable to many different types of subsidies given to many different industries operating under vastly differing circumstances must focus on the commonality in the mechanisms that determine the environmental effects of removing a subsidy. As a consequence, it inevitably will miss several factors that may be decisive, or conversely, will contain items that are not relevant with respect to a particular subsidy. Therefore a checklist cannot substitute for a more thorough analysis that would reveal elements missed in the checklist and would give a much more reliable picture of the effects of removing that subsidy.

In summary, if properly developed, the checklist can:

- serve as a "quick scan", allowing governments to concentrate on those subsidies for which removal would most likely result in environmental gains;

- help in identifying important elements that should go into a more thorough analysis; and

- help governments claiming justifiable environmental benefits, and avoiding unjustifiable ones. The checklist should allow identifying reinforcing and mitigating factors that together determine the final outcomes of subsidy removal right from the start.

## *Limitations of the checklist and its underlying reasoning*

Ideally, the effects of subsidy removal should be estimated using general or at least partial equilibrium models, taking the responses of other sectors into account. The checklist, by contrast, only enumerates economic characteristics of subsidies that may serve as predictors for first order effects on those industries that are directly affected by the removal of a certain subsidy. The reasoning behind the checklist ignores wider macro-economic implications, such as the effects of subsidy removal on governments' budgets and consumers' incomes and their effects on the economy when recycled.

Subsidies have effects on international trade and therefore on the geographical distribution of economic activities. Removing subsidies in one country therefore will lead to effects in other countries. Analysing the full effects of subsidy removal should include these effects. This is a considerable extension of the analysis, compared to a purely national one. On the other hand, the effects of subsidy removal on these extensions would basically entail the same elements as a national analysis, only being applied at more markets and more (and different) economic and environmental circumstances. Therefore the checklist is only developed having a national analysis in mind. This means, however, that possible effects of the international trade regime on trade flows once a subsidy is removed, have been ignored.

The development of a checklist should ideally be based on a thorough meta analysis of *ex ante* and preferably *ex post* evaluations of subsidy removal, eliminating all the effects of differences in data and methodologies applied in those case studies. This, being a gigantic task, is beyond the scope of this paper. Instead the reasoning in this paper and the checklist is mainly based on previous OECD work (notably OECD, 1997 a,b, c and d; OECD, 1998, 1999a, b; OECD 2002, and the literature cited in these studies) and basic micro-economic theory.

No doubt the attained results are provisional and leave ample room for improvement and refinement.

## Subsidy – environment linkages

The links between subsidies and their environmental effects are very complex. These links vary from being very direct, *e.g.* if the subsidy is conditional on the production or use of a particular substance that causes environmental harm, while cleaner alternatives are available, to very indirect, if the subsidy is decoupled from production levels. The whole exercise boils down to identifying the factors that determine the directness of the links between removing a subsidy and its environmental consequences. The checklist focuses on the following.

- *A subsidy changes the relative volumes of economic activities and, potentially, emissions and rates of exploitation.* A subsidy increases revenues or reduces costs of the recipient sector, or may even decisive for starting the economic activity in the first place. As a result, at least the composition of (domestic) production and consumption will change. Generally speaking the subsidised economic activity will expand and others will contract (unless the subsidy was granted to a monopoly). The degree to which this happens depends on the final incidence of the subsidy, which in turn depends on numerous elasticities of demand and supply on both factor and product markets. Such a shift in the composition of production and consumption may have significant environmental consequences (even if the total of production would not change), due to the vast differences in resource needs and pollution between industries.

- *The competitiveness of the subsidised sector may also be influenced by technical change.* In the long run, autonomous technical change as well as changes in market conditions may also change the relative competitiveness of the subsidised and non-subsidised industries. Maintaining the competitiveness of an industry through subsidisation may very well be an uphill fight, defending the industry against ever more efficient competitors. This also applies to subsidies that previously have been installed to favour environmentally benign modes of production. As a result, removing a long-standing subsidy may free the way to the application of novel technologies, which introduction have been blocked by the subsidy. This (only) yields benefits for the environment if the new technologies are more environmentally benign, which, in turn, will be influenced by the effectiveness of environmental policy.

146

- *The effects of subsidy removal on emissions or rates of depletion depend also on the prevailing "policy filter".* Subsidisation takes place within a prevailing environmental policy context. This context may consist of a set of environmental measures such as the requirement to adhere to a set of best available technologies (BAT) or other measures that prescribe certain modes of production, like sustainable forestry, or maximum rates of exploitation or production. For example, if BAT requirements prescribe flue-gas desulphurisation, the removal of a subsidy that would lead to an increase of the use of sulphur-rich fuels would have a much smaller effect on tonnes of $SO_2$ emissions than if those requirements were absent. Likewise, removing a subsidy to a fishery may have no effect on fish stocks, if there is a management regime in place that already effectively prevents over-fishing. Other elements of the policy filter would include all other quantity restrictions such as the maximum capacity of infrastructure (in a given period), or planning and zoning requirements.

- *The resulting changes in emissions and rates of exploitation due to subsidy removal may improve the (use) values of the environment.* The remaining changes in emissions and exploitation rates due to subsidy removal affect the environment, if the subsidy had environmental effects to begin with (that is, if its detrimental environmental effects had not already been eliminated by policy decisions, or other constraints). This depends on the site-specific assimilative capacity or resilience of the environment (dose response relations). Next, changes in the environment will influence the use values of the environment, which feeds back into the economic structure.

- *Effects of existing subsidies on the (use) values of the environment may constitute a political argument to remove that subsidy.* The state of the environment may lead governments to explore whether removing subsidies would improve the environment. Typically this would entail drafting a list of existing subsidies that are likely to cause environmental harm. The next step would be to identify those subsidies that should be removed on environmental grounds. In the majority of cases the decision to remove a subsidy needs a firm argumentation. The environmental case must be stronger the less there are other arguments like the ineffectiveness of subsidies to achieve other policy objectives (such as increased income or employment or both).

### The basic line of reasoning

The basic line of argument concerning the items that should go into the checklist is that removing subsidies will have the largest environmental

147

impacts if they directly affect the production and use of natural resources or emissions. The directness of the link between the environment (exploitation rates of resources or emissions, or both) and the subsidised activity depends on:

- Whether the subsidy to-be-removed is conditional on input or output levels. If not, its removal would affect relative incomes, but not having significant environmental impacts (only those that are affected by changes in relative incomes).

- The input/environment ratio within the subsidised economic activity, which in turn depends on the availability of alternative modes of production. If this ratio is invariable [*e.g.* (Carbon content of the energy used)/($CO_2$-emissions)] removing subsidies to carbon containing fuels would be in order. If the ratio is variable, removing the subsidy or intensifying environmental policy should be considered.

- The output/environment ratio of the subsidised industry, which also depends on the availability of alternative modes of production. If this ratio is variable only within close limits (*e.g.* in the case of a capital intensive industry), removing the subsidy to output would have significant effects on pollution or resource exploitation. Otherwise other measures of environmental policy would be the preferred option.

- The availability of close substitutes for the products of the subsidised industry.

The way subsidies influence technical change is of great importance, especially in the long run, as the directness of the link between the subsidy and the environment depends strongly on the availability of alternatives. In this respect a distinction is made between removing subsidies that influence day to day decisions (their removal leading to a continuous new incentive to technical change — resource productivity) and removing subsidies that influence one-off decisions (their removal eliminating the opportunity to install environmentally benign technologies that are available at the time subsidisation starts, but also avoiding that technologies that are not so good after all are being locked-in for a considerable period of time). This distinction coincides with subsidies to environmentally relevant variable costs (energy, materials, water) exercising a continuous disincentive to increasing resource productivity on the one hand and subsidies to capital equipment that can only use a particular input (which make them subsidies to that particular input in disguise), but with a discontinuous disincentive to technical change and other input subsidies, on the other.

## Lessons from previous work

Previous OECD work as well as (many) other case studies yield valuable insights on factors that are particularly important for developing a checklist. The primary lesson is that "details matter". On a less lofty level, other lessons have been learnt from previous case studies; lessons that when stripped from the specific circumstances from which they are drawn, may be applicable (in various degree) to other cases and are useful as to point at items that should be included in the checklist.

- The linkages between a subsidy and its environmental effects are complex. As a consequence, a subsidy to an economic activity that gives rise to significant emissions is not necessarily an environmentally damaging one. It is essential to analyse the consequences of subsidy removal and the alternatives that will benefit from it.

- The final incidence of subsidies can differ strongly from their initial impacts. Subsidies tend to be passed on to suppliers and customers, according to price elasticities of demand and supply. To assess the environmental effects of subsidy removal therefore must entail an analysis of the cluster of economic activities that is linked by input-output relations and is affected by the subsidy.

- Subsidies are not deployed in isolation. Most often they are part of more comprehensive sectoral policies, aimed at, for example, maintaining certain production or employment levels or at restructuring the sector without too much social hardship. Such policy packages typically contain many more policy measures than just subsidies, such as institutional arrangements, planning and zoning requirements, training. Arguably a number of those measures will lead to subsidisation under a broad definition.

- Financial support may be the source or the outcome of a policy package. Government brokered contracts deployed in for example coal subsidy programmes, basically stipulate obligatory purchases from domestic suppliers, leading to higher consumer prices and subsidisation of the coal industry (Steenblik and Coryannakis, 1995).

- Other examples of possible accompanying measures that influence the effects of subsidies or their removal are environmental management regimes and other elements of the "policy filter" mentioned above. If, for example, subsidies to fisheries are removed while catches are limited by other measures, or when certain types of subsidies to road or energy are removed while infrastructure is a limiting factor, the effects of removal may not be significant (Hannesson, 2001; Roy, 2000).

- Moreover, subsidies also operate under even more general conditions such as the prevailing taxation regimes. As Chen (OECD, 1999) and Pillet (OECD, 1999) have pointed out, the same subsidy would lead to different effects on marginal costs, if applied under different taxation regimes. Great care must be taken if one wants to transpose the results of one subsidy study to another tax jurisdiction.

- Assessing the consequences of introducing or removing subsidies implies that one has to compare a factual with an unknown counterfactual situation that serves as a benchmark. The assumptions underlying the counterfactual situation may have strong effects on the outcomes. Assume a subsidy that favours a certain technology (such as coal-fired power generation). That subsidy will depress the deployment of new technologies. Answering the question what would happen if the subsidy were to be removed, implies answering the question what technologies if any, would have replaced coal-fired power generation. Since that is a difficult question to answer, even *ex post* analyses of subsidy removal tend to be based on arbitrary assumptions underlying the counterfactual situation (Annex 1, item 2). The longer the subsidy has been in place, the larger the potential effects of missed technical improvements tend to be.

- Changing subsidies related to production or input levels into subsidies that are decoupled (from inputs and outputs) may not change things very much. Subsidies get capitalised in the price of the least elastic factor of production, land for example in the case of agriculture. Removing a subsidy therefore will lower the price of that production factor, leading to a more extensive use of it. However, if that subsidy is replaced by another, this new subsidy will get capitalised in the price of the same production factor. As a consequence, removing a subsidy to for example irrigation water (conditional on input use) and replacing it with a subsidy based on historical entitlements (decoupled from actual input or production levels), may not change the price of land. As a result, production will remain as land intensive as it was, possibly leading to the same, levels of irrigation water use (see, for example, Rainelli, 1998).

- Liberalising trade may not have the opposite effect of installing subsidies. A study on the effects of liberalising trade in agriculture on Dutch agriculture (Massink and Meester, 2002) reveals that trade liberalisation would lead to significant income transfers, changes in the composition of Dutch agricultural production and to a further *intensification* of agriculture, this while subsidisation is widely believed to have had increased intensification.

- Subsidies, especially to capital intensive industries, may lead to strong lock-in effects. Once such an industry has established or expanded its capacity, not utilising that capacity may lead to high costs. Indeed continuing subsidisation may be cheaper than not recuperating the sunk costs, but not more efficient in the long run (Naughten *et al.*, 1997 in OECD, 1997*b*).

- Pollution and resource use are parts of substance flows through the economy. In fact all environmental effects stem from substance flows (Ayres and Ayres, 1996). Subsidies to energy carriers and materials, including water are the most directly linked to substance flows. Subsidies to technologies that are bound to use particular energy carriers or materials may also be very closely linked to substance flows. Subsidies that leave room for choosing more environmentally benign modes of production may be less detrimental for the environment, provided an effective environmental policy that prevents choices for ever more damaging options.

- Subsidies may have different initial points of impact, such as output, input and profits and income. Initial points of impact matter for two reasons. Subsidies to inputs affect different markets than subsidies to outputs or profits and income (OECD, 2001b). Generally speaking, subsidies that directly impact materials flows have more direct effects on forward linkages than subsidies to output or profits and income. (It should be noted that such subsidies leave less options for more benign modes of production than subsidies to output or income.) Second, if input subsidies are conditional on the use of particular energy carriers or materials (including water), or particular types of capital equipment that require only certain types of energy carriers or materials, they will discourage materials and energy saving, on which the success of environmental policy is highly dependent.

- Subsidies tend to cast technologies in stone, especially if they are meant to shelter industries that deploy technologies that are not economically viable. Even subsidies that favour new and better technologies may lock-in technologies that in the long run may prove to be inferior to even newer and better non subsidised technologies.

# Merging theory with evidence

## *Introduction*

Subsidies are always conditional on something, be it output, inputs, profits and income, or factors that influence demand. The various types of conditionality lead to different points of impact of the subsidy. Different points of impact in turn, lead to different responses of the subsidised firms. Generally, the effects of subsidy removal depend strongly on the overall policy setting, as well as circumstances.

Before dealing with the conditionality of a number of subsidy types, two general observations should be made.

- Subsidies may have lock-in effects, meaning that they can cast technologies in stone by protecting relatively "dirty" technologies. Since the success of environmental policy greatly depends on the development and deployment of new more environmentally benign technologies, this is an important source of environmental harm done by certain types of subsidies.

- Economic theory suggests that a firm's responses to changes in variable (marginal) costs differ from those in fixed costs.

## *The lock-in effect*

Reducing the environmental impacts of economic activities depends on reducing volumes of production and reducing emissions or input requirements per unit of production.[3] The latter is often called "decoupling". Basically, decoupling can be achieved by: increasing resource efficiency ("making more with less"), deploying abatement (end-of-pipe technologies), or both. These strategies are described in some more detail in Table 1 (OECD, 1998).

All of the strategies delineated in the table mentioned above have strong and weak points. Which strategy will be the best solution in any given situation will depend largely on the particular circumstances of the environmental problem it is required to address. Sometimes the choice of available strategies will be limited. Preventing pollution and waste from being generated (through process integrated solutions) is often cheaper than trying to reduce their toxicity and dispose of them after their generation; hence, in general, increasing resource productivity is more cost effective than end-of-pipe technologies (there are exceptions). Where there is dissipative use of materials (*e.g.* detergents, fertilizer, pesticides), pollution prevention may even be the only option to reduce pollution levels.

**Table 1. A typology of the main technological strategies**
**of environmental policy**

| Category | Main strategies of environmental policy | Examples |
|---|---|---|
| *End-of-Pipe Treatment* (Pollution Control) | *Reducing the toxicity of pollution and waste*<br><br>Transforming pollution and waste into emissions and waste streams that are less hazardous, or managing them in a more environmentally-benign manner | Waste water treatment, flue-gas desulphurisation, remediation activities, sequestration and disposal of waste in "safe" disposal sites |
| *Increasing Resource Productivity* (Pollution Prevention) | *Dematerialisation* More efficient use of a given material for a given function | Energy saving measures, less fertiliser and/or pesticide use per unit of agricultural output, increased vehicle fuel efficiency of (including the reduction of vehicles weight), micro-miniaturisation in the electronics industry |
| | *Materials Substitution* Substitution of a given material by another, less hazardous (including less energy -intensive) one | Substitution of glass or aluminium fibre for copper wire, replacement of CFCs by other materials, use of less malign pesticides, use of aluminium or other light weight materials in vehicles construction |
| | *Recycling* Repair, re-use, remanufacturing and recycling of products | Recovery of metals from discarded products, recycling of paper and glass, energy recovery by incineration of discarded products |
| | *Waste Mining* Recovery of materials from production waste | Recovery of elemental sulphur from flue-gas desulphurisation, recovery of limestone from scrubber waste, recovery of fertiliser by applying closed production systems in agriculture |

*Source:* OECD (1998), adapted from Ayres and Ayres (1996).

The bottom line is that success in environmental policy is largely dependent on changes in substance flows through the economy. In consequence, subsidies that stifle technical change are likely to harm the environment in the longer run, provided that environmental policy ensures that new technologies compare favourably with the older ones in their environmental effects. The more a subsidy fixates on a particular technology, the more suspect it is.[4] These subsidies include subsidies to a particular input and subsidies to a particular type of capital good. Note that often there is a rather close link between a particular type of machinery and the inputs that are suitable for that machinery (*e.g.* type of machinery and the fuel it runs on). Subsidies that favour certain technologies over others add to the "lock-in effect".[5] The longer a subsidy is in place, the stronger it will add to the lock-in effect.

It is difficult to assess lock-in effects quantitatively, since one has to compare a "with-situation" with a counterfactual "without-situation". But subsidies that are maintained for a long period are much more likely to have strong lock-in effects, especially when they also directly influence the choice of materials and energy.

### The importance of distinguishing between variable and marginal costs

Standard economic theory tells us that *output* is determined by the equalisation of marginal costs and marginal revenues: the price of the product. *Profitability* is determined by the difference between average costs and average revenues: the price of the product. The equality of minimum average costs and marginal costs determines the *optimal scale of the firm and the optimal offer price* at the same token. Hence subsidies to fixed costs have different effects on total quantities used or produced by the entire industry compared to subsidies to variable costs. Over the long run, however, all costs are variable and these differences will disappear.

There are, however four reasons to distinguish between subsidies to variable costs on one hand and to fixed costs on the other.

- *Short and long term versus long term effects only:* Removing subsidies to variable costs increase *marginal costs*. This immediately affects day-to-day production decisions, since only operations which revenues exceed marginal costs increase profits or reduce losses. Removing subsidies to fixed costs (*i.e.* subsidies that lower the cost of capital, *e.g.* low interest loans, the costs of buildings, capital equipment, land), by contrast, generally affects only *new investments* in the industry, since one cannot undo past acquisitions of assets. As a result, their effect will kick in only gradually.[6] Their full effects may take even decades to materialise.

- *Continuous versus discontinuous change:* Removing subsidies to materials and energy can work only into one direction: encouraging resource efficiency.[7] The effect will be *continuous,* spurring the emergence of ever more resource efficient modes of production. This is likely to have large environmental impacts since the industries engaged in the early phases of production (extraction, energy and materials production) are among the highest polluting industries. By contrast, removing subsidies to capital equipment affects "one-off" investment decisions and fixates technical change over the life times of the subsidised capital goods.

- *Always right, or sometimes right:* Whereas the removal of subsidies to environmentally relevant variable cost always work in the right direction, removing subsidies to fixed costs, in particular capital equipment, may temporarily damage the environment (if they favour environmentally more benign modes of production), or conversely improve the environment (if they favour relatively "dirty" modes of production). Note that the positive effect is likely to be temporarily, because autonomous technical change eventually may render modes of production that once were environmentally benign into ones that are relatively "dirty".

- *Closeness of the link between the subsidy and the environment:* The link between energy and materials use on the one hand (categories of variable costs), and pollution and exploitation of natural resources on the other, is more direct than the link between fixed costs and environmental impacts, unless the subsidy is conditional on the deployment of a narrowly defined type of capital equipment that uses only one specific type of material or fuel. Arguably then it is an indirect subsidy to that input. An example in case would be a subsidy to a coal-fired power plant. Such plants are very capital intensive, but coal is a cheap fuel compared to gas. Subsidising the coal-fired plant therefore can be seen as an indirect subsidy to coal to the detriment of the cleaner fuel, gas. Subsidies to types of fixed costs that do not implicitly lock-in modes of production, such as subsidies to land, buildings and the cost of capital, leave the firm choices for environmentally more benign modes of production while being subsidised. Removing such subsidies is likely to have comparatively small beneficial effects.

As a rule of the thumb, removing subsidies to environmentally relevant variable costs (materials, energy, water) have a greater immediate impact on the environment than subsidies to fixed costs. This also applies to subsidies to types of fixed costs that implicitly lock in the use of certain materials and energy carriers.

### Conditionality: the main points of impact

Subsidies are always conditional on something. The various types of conditionality or points of impact (Table 2) of the subsidies may lead to different responses of producers and consumers with respect to their modes of production, production and consumption levels and as a consequence to differences in the changes in levels of pollution and rates of exploitation. The purpose of this section is to explore the differences in likely responses of firms due to removing subsidies that have different points of impact.

Usually the following broad categories of points of impact are distinguished: output, input, and profits and income.[8] Such a characterisation always has arbitrary elements, because details of the subsidies at hand are not easily captured in such broad categories. Moreover, at the end of the day, all subsidies translate into either revenue increases or cost reductions. The usual break-down of subsidies, however, highlights some important differences in subsidies: revenue increases conditional on the volume of production (output); revenue increases irrespective of volumes produced (profit and income); and production cost reductions (input use).

We have introduced another criterion, namely points of impact that lie "within the firm" (affecting the individual firm's own cost and revenue structure directly) and "outside the firm" (affecting demand and thereby indirectly its revenues). In the first case, the firms avail themselves on the subsidy by making certain choices of its own, in the latter case the subsidies benefit the industry collectively, giving the firm less influence on the volume of the subsidised product to be produced. In terms of economic analysis, in the first case the changes are along the demand curve, whereas in the latter case the demand curves themselves shift.

156

## Table 2. Main points of impact / support conditionality

| Categories | Main initial points of impact | Effects on sales, costs and rent |
|---|---|---|
| *Within the firm[1] (affecting costs and revenues of the firm that avails itself on the subsidy)* | | |
| **Output** | Market price support<br>Border protection<br>Market access restrictions<br>Government brokered contract<br>Deficiency payments and sales premiums | Creates revenues proportional to actual production volumes (increase production levels) |
| | Production quota | Off-sets production increase; creates rents (market value of quota) |
| **Input use** | Materials, energy<br>Short-lived equipment | Reduces variable costs |
| | Particular types of fixed capital<br>Access to natural resources below opportunity costs | Reduces variable or fixed costs, or both |
| **Profit and income** | Historical entitlements<br>Preferential low rates of income taxes<br>Preferential low rates of capital taxes<br>Debt write-off<br>Allowing insufficient provision for future environmental liabilities<br>Exemptions from (environmental) standards<br>Start of an operation | Creates revenues, irrespective of actual production volumes (increases profits)[2] |
| | Low rate of return requirements | Reduces fixed costs and revenues |
| *Outside the firm[1] (increasing demand, thereby affecting revenues of the industry collectively)* | | |
| **Demand** | Low rates of VAT<br>Marketing and promotion by government<br>Provision of government produced infrastructure below costs | Stimulates demand |

1. By "firm" we mean an organisation producing a certain product. In case of vertical integration, a firm in the judicial sense may contain several "firms" we are referring to in this table.
2. Such subsidies include "existence subsidies", which purpose is to maintain subsidised activities without these producing anything for the market (but for producing non-marketable values).
*Source*: Adapted from OECD (1998).

### *Removing a subsidy conditional to quantity of output*

*Market price support,* which represents a very important part of subsidies granted (agriculture, fisheries, coal), is either given to ensure certain output levels of domestic production that exceed volumes or to ensure a certain price level above the level without the market price support, or both. Removing such subsidies will reduce output of the previously subsidised product. If no change in technology occurs, this reduction equals the decrease in pollution or resource exploitation associated with the previously subsidised economic activity. At the same time, a proportionate reduction is to be expected in the supplying industries, leading to smaller environmental impacts. Removing market price support will lead to shifts in the geographical distribution of production locations with the associated changes in local environmental quality.

All volume effects are dependent on both price elasticity of demand and price elasticity of supply of the subsidised product. The largest effects occur if both demand and supply elasticities are large. Medium effects would result if either one elasticity is large and the other is small (OECD, 1998, Part II and Annex 2). The net effect on the environment depends also on what products will replace the previously subsidised ones. For example, what alternative crops will be grown, what alternative species will be caught, and would the previously subsidised coal be replaced by imported coal or by an entirely different fuel?

Removing output subsidies leads to a loss of producers' surplus and a decrease of production volumes (unless the latter continue to be limited by quotas or other environmental management regimes). In agriculture this is likely to lower the prices of farm land that (if sufficiently large, and translated into rents) may in turn stimulate farmers to produce less intensively. In other sectors the prices of other factors that have an inelastic supply will decrease. Usually, however, such second order effects are relatively small.

Subsidies (not only market price support) are not applied in a vacuum. In a number of cases they are accompanied by various production limitations such as: exploitation or production quotas (*e.g.* in agriculture, fisheries, forestry); limitations of the available infrastructure (*e.g.* in energy and transport); planning and zoning requirements (*e.g.* in industry, agriculture, energy, transport); pollution limits (all sectors). If those limitations are maintained, it may be them that determine the overall effect of subsidy removal. This will be the case if for example production limits have been set to avoid over production even at the higher prices that result from market price support (such a as milk or fish quota). By contrast, removing both the subsidy together with the production limit will result in an increase in production volumes, if the production limit was below production limits that correspond with market equilibrium after subsidy and production limit removal.[9]

*Deficiency payments and sales premiums*, also being mechanisms to bridge the gap between a politically determined price and the market price, have similar effects on production volumes as market price support.

### *Removing a subsidy to input use*

*Materials (including water), energy.* Removing these subsidies is likely to have substantial environmental benefits. Their removal increases variable cost, which effects are felt immediately and continuously; remove the lock-in effects that block developments towards more resource productivity which in turn; reducing the environmental impacts of the extracting, energy producing and materials producing industries.

*Short lived equipment.* Removing these subsidies likewise increases variable costs. Whether they have the wider effects on resource efficiency that characterise the removal of subsidies to energy and materials, depends on the degree to which they are linked to specific materials or energy uses.

*Capital equipment.* Removing these subsidies will slow down new investments, which could have a *negative* impact on the environment if those new investments would be more environmentally benign. Such a subsidy removal generally applies to new investments only, therefore the full effects will be felt only in the long run, if a significant portion of the old investments have been replaced by new (non-subsidised and therefore more expensive) equipment. Whether the environment will benefit from higher costs of equipment in the long run, depends on two other factors as well: its effect on total production levels and substitution of factors of production towards more labour or more materials inputs, or both. Removing such subsidies may also have environmentally beneficial effects if the previously subsidised capital equipment has become relatively environmentally harmful. The more the previous subsidy has been conditional on narrowly defined types of equipment and the longer it has been in place, the more it is likely to have locked-in particular presently "dirty" technologies. Removal of such subsidies are to be expected to have stronger beneficial effects than the removal of subsidies that applied to broadly defined categories of equipment.

*Access to natural resources below opportunity costs (e.g.* exploitation concessions below opportunity costs — forestry, mining, water extraction, etc., government purchased access to foreign owned fishing grounds). Removing such subsidies decreases the rates of exploitation of the natural resources concerned. They may have an immediate effect (*e.g.* in the case governments no longer paying for access to foreign fishing grounds) or a long-term effect (*e.g.* if governments sell new concessions at higher prices). Removing such subsidies often will have a decisive effect on the start or the continuation of the affected economic activity.

*Low interest loans.* Low interest loans are a subsidy to capital. Usually they will reduce the (sunk) cost of fixed assets and they may lower the internal rate of discount. They, however also make funds available for other acquisitions. Whether their removal results in an increase of fixed or variable costs is difficult to determine. Since these subsidies (if not conditional on specific types of equipment) leave the firm free in choosing more environmentally benign modes of production, they may not have been as environmentally damaging as their effects on production volumes might suggest. As a consequence, it is more difficult to assess beforehand whether their removal would benefit the environment. More detailed analysis would be necessary.

*Research and development.* Assessing the effects of removing these subsidies also requires more detailed analyses. On the environmentally beneficial side, subsidies to research and development can be directed towards environmentally more benign production modes. On the other hand they may postpone a change to fundamentally different technologies that are even more benign. Worse even, if these subsidies would be sufficiently large that they work like a subsidy to operating costs, while conditional on the prevailing line of operations, they are likely to have serious lock-in effects. The effects of removing these subsidies on fixed or variable costs are difficult to determine (during the research and development stage, as well as when the results of the research and development efforts are put into practice).

### Removing a subsidy to profits and income

*Historical entitlements.* These subsidies are independent on actual production volumes. However, they get capitalised in the prices of factors of production in inelastic supply such as land, in which case removing them may have a downwards effect on these factors of production and might change modes of production and production levels. Assessing the environmental effects of removing these subsidies requires a rather detailed analysis, taking the details of production functions of firms into account.

*Preferential low rates of income or capital taxation and debt write offs.* Such subsidies improve the *profitability* of the firms concerned (assuming that they are not also conditional on particular technologies and input uses) and will prolong the life span of firms that are not economically viable in the absence of these subsidies. Consequently, removing them will make the least efficient firms (possibly also the most polluting ones) leave the sector, possibly reducing the total output of the sector with favourable environmental consequences (if the reduction in supply is not filled with supply from other even more polluting or resource inefficient firms). Firms that use environmentally more benign processes may enter the industry, thus removing the lock-in effects of subsidies to profits and income. Again, we are faced with a mixed bag of potential outcomes and rather detailed research is needed to establish the environmental effects of removing these subsidies.

*Allowing insufficient provision for future liabilities and exemptions from (environmental) standards.* Removing these subsidies is likely to have strong beneficial effects on the environment. They contain examples of measures to shore up the profitability of economic activities that otherwise would not have been economically viable, deliberately at the expense of the environment. Removing exemptions from environmental standards may increase marginal costs.

*Start of an operation.* In order to lure an investor to start an operation, apart form other subsidies, a lump sum subsidy may be granted. No longer giving them would reduce investments in that particular jurisdiction. Of course the (local) environmental effects depend on the nature and scale of that operation. The effects of removing such subsidies, therefore, are hard to predict.

*Low rate of return requirements.* These subsidies are applied to government owned utilities forcing producers to reduce their offer prices, most often in conjunction with low interest loans. They serve as a means to pass on preferential the low interest rates to consumers. In fact they lower the internal discount rate for the entire operations (or reduce the break-even price). Removing them will result in a shift to less capital intensive, and therefore more flexible technologies with higher rates of return. Depending on the environmental characteristics of the alternative production processes, removing low rate of return requirements may have beneficial or adverse effects on the environment. It should be noted, however, that investments with shorter economic life spans, open the way to more frequent adaptations to new technological options, and possibly to their development.

### Removing a subsidy that increases demand

*Preferential low VAT rates, the provision of infrastructure below costs as well as other governments services below (long term marginal) costs, such as government paid marketing and product promotion.* Removing these subsidies (to consumers) does not affect the subsidised firms directly but decrease the demand for their products. If the supply curve is inelastic, a decrease in demand due to the removal of the subsidy will have little effect. This could be the case when governments decide to have road users to pay more for using congested roads, while there are also no or limited possibilities to increase the capacity of other modes of transport. In the first case, congestion will have depressed demand, while being subsidised. If the roads were not congested, the effect of charging more for the use of infrastructure, is likely to be significantly larger.

## Conclusions

Subsidy removal has a larger impact if: the subsidies have been implemented for a long time; they have been targeted at environmentally relevant variable costs; they have had (upstream) effects on industries that are relatively polluting or resource intensive by themselves and have been applied to existing production capacity, not just new additions. Subsidy removal, by contrast, has lesser impact if: there are other environmental constraints that are not removed together with the subsidy; they have been in place for a short time; they have not affected relatively polluting or resource intensive sectors. In Table 3 the results of the previous analysis are summarised in more detail.

## Developing the checklist

### Introduction

As stated before, the checklist does not contain elements that determine whether one is dealing with a subsidy or not, neither does it contain items that indicate the nature and severity of the environmental damage (pollution or resource depletion). The checklist only helps in answering the question of whether the removal of a subsidy is likely to result in environmental benefits.

The subsidy removal affects prices and volumes produced and may reverse some directions in technical change that have been stimulated by the subsidy. Next the effects of subsidies may have been mitigated or reinforced by accompanying policy measures (that include building of infrastructure). Finally, "autonomous" technical change may have resulted in environmentally more benign alternatives the deployment of which may have been prevented by the subsidy. Following this overall view, three clusters of questions suggest themselves:

- What restrictions to production, pollution or resource depletion levels result from the policy filter, and of course, what will happen to the policy filter once the subsidies are removed.

- What technologies and products are likely to replace the previously subsidised products and modes of production, and subsequently how do the environmental profiles of these competing products and modes of production compare with those of the previously subsidised ones.

162

**Table 3. Overview of to be expected effects of subsidy removal**

| | | Environmental effects[1] | | |
|---|---|---|---|---|
| Categories | Main points of impact | Short term[2] reduction in emissions or rates of exploitation *due to:* | Long term[2] reduction in emissions or rates of exploitation *due to:* | Remarks |
| **Output** | Market price support. Deficiency payments. Sales premiums. | Lower production levels. Same as above. Same as above. | Lower production levels. Same as above. Same as above. | Consumer prices will drop, in spite of lower production levels. Less input requirements may lead to strong environmental effects in the production of materials and energy phase. Production may shift to areas of low cost production, leading to a possible displacement of the environmental burden. |
| **Input use** | Materials, energy. | Higher marginal costs of all subsidised "firms"; immediate discontinuation of some production activities. Exit of the least efficient production units, if marginal revenues drop below marginal costs. | Disappearance of the lock-in effect, which frees the way to substitution and savings on inputs. If accompanied by effective environmental policies this creates a window of opportunities for environmental improvement.[3] | Strong effects may be expected due to reductions in the production of materials and energy or rates of exploitation that often are relatively environmentally harmful. |
| | Short lived equipment. | Same as above. | Same as above | |

163

| Categories | Main points of impact | Short term[2] reduction in emissions or rates of exploitation *due to* | Long term[2] reduction in emissions or rates of exploitation *due to* | Remarks |
|---|---|---|---|---|
| **Input use** *(continued)* | Particular types of fixed capital. | Exit of the least efficient production units, if marginal revenues drop below marginal costs. | Disappearance of the lock-in effect, depending on the specificity and duration of the conditionality. | If substitution of capital equipment opens the way to more efficient use of materials or energy (or less harmful ones), strong effects upstream may be expected. |
| | Access to natural resources. | Increases the price of natural resources for downstream users, increase their resource efficiency. | Higher barrier to entry or disappearance of the least efficient production units, or both. | Strong effects on entry with possibly large beneficial effects on rates of depletion. |
| | Low interest loans. | Possibly a (limited) effect on marginal costs. | Higher barrier to entry or disappearance of the least efficient production units, or both. | |
| | Research and development. | | Deployment of environmentally more benign technologies, if accompanied with effective environmental targets. | |
| | | | | If the subsidy is large, it may be an exploitation subsidy to capital costs in disguise. In those cases, the effects are unclear. |
| **Profit and income**[4] | Preferential low rates of income taxes. | Possibly somewhat lower marginal costs. If so, exit of the least efficient production units, if marginal revenues drop below marginal costs. | Higher barrier to entry. Higher prices reduce demand. | |
| | Preferential low rates of capital taxes. | The same as above. | The same as above. | |
| | Debt write off. | The same as above, unless it is a one-off write off. | The same as above, unless it is a one-off write off. | |

| Categories | Main points of impact | Short term[2] reduction in emissions or rates of exploitation *due to* | Long term[2] reduction in emissions or rates of exploitation *due to* | Remarks |
|---|---|---|---|---|
| **Profit and income** (*continued*) | Allowing insufficient provision for future environmental liabilities. | Exit of the least efficient production units, if marginal revenues drop below marginal costs. | Higher consumer prices and more environmentally benign modes of production. | |
| | Exemptions from (environmental) standards. | Same as above. | Same as above. | |
| | Low rate of return requirements. | | Higher consumer prices and higher internal discount rates. The latter shortens the planning horizon of the "firm" and thereby the lock-in effect. | |
| **Demand** | Low rates of VAT. | Exit of the least efficient production units, if marginal revenues drop below marginal costs | Undetermined, since dependent on externalities. | Some "up stream" effects may be expected. |
| | Marketing and promotion by government. | Same as above | Same as above. | Same as above. |
| | Provision of infrastructure below costs. | Same as above | The same as above. More decentralised production close to the place of consumption; different technologies. | The environmental effects depend also on site specific environmental conditions. |

1. As stated before, elements of the policy filter (quota, limitations in infrastructure) may become, or remain the limiting factors to production and thereby to the environmental effects of subsidy removal. In this table, this is ignored.
2. In the sort run, technology remains the same. That is, there is no substitution between factors of production or inputs for that matter.
3. Choosing a particular input often casts the technology in stone and vice versa.
4. Removal of subsidies based on historical entitlements, or direct payments to producers in exchange for production(modes) that are environmentally beneficial have been omitted from the table, because such removal is likely to damage the environment.

- What are the likely the responses of the previously subsidised industries in terms of production volumes, rates of exploitation of natural resources. This depends on size and conditionality of the subsidy as well as the distribution of market power.

This results in the following simple flowchart that underlies the checklist (Figure 1). First, it should be investigated if other restrictions (either politically or technical in nature) that counteract the subsidy removal will remain in place. If so, subsidy removal will have no or a limited effect. Second, it should be investigated whether there are environmentally more benign alternatives available in the short and long term. Long-term availability may be a matter of judgement. If so, the third step would be to look into the subsidy itself to determine what precisely is the conditionality of the subsidy and what the responses of the firms will be if the subsidy were to be removed. This seems, analytically, the most demanding task. This more detailed analysis will also reveal whether subsidy removal will be difficult to predict because of market power. Developing a checklist for such cases was beyond the scope of this paper.

Step 3, investigating the role of conditionality (initial points of impact) on the directness of the link between subsidy removal and its environmental effects is based on the basic reasoning laid down above. Summarising the results of those sections, Step 3 of the checklist emphasises the following issues:

- Availability and potential environmental impacts of close substitutes for the products of the subsidised activities, once the subsidisation stops, and that, by consequence, are likely to replace (some of the) previously subsidised products.

- The forward and backward linkages of the industry that loses a subsidy.

- The restoration of incentives to continuous technical change by subsidy removal. Hence items are included to identify subsidies that are contingent on environmentally relevant categories of variable costs (energy, materials, water).

- Identifying subsidies to capital equipment that are implicit subsidies to certain inputs that are environmentally relevant.

- The effects of subsidisation on one-off decisions such as starting an operation or investing in capital equipment with a long life span. These decisions can have large environmental effects, but whether they are detrimental or beneficial to the environment depends on the alternatives that may come to the market after the subsidy has been granted. Such subsidies may lock in technologies that are not so "clean" after all.

- Identifying subsidies which removal would influence day-to-day decisions and would have an immediate effect on the environment and conversely subsidies which removal would affect decisions that only gradually would affect the environment.

## Figure 1. Subsidy removal checklist

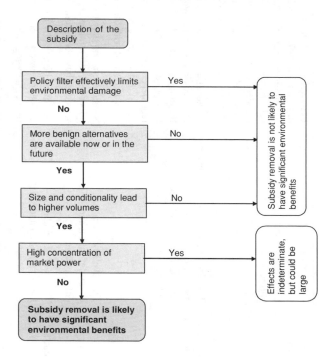

The items in the checklist (Table 4) are meant to facilitate answering the above mentioned three clusters of questions. Applying a checklist like the one developed here serves as a "quick scan". More definite answers can only be arrived at, applying more detailed analyses preferably using general equilibrium models. In fact, several items under step 3 can only be answered more or less convincingly by applying such models. The checklist may be of some help in deciding whether such more elaborate analyses are required and what items should be included. Since the effects of subsidies depend on so many factors, this first attempt to arrive at a checklist is likely not to be complete.

**Table 4. Factors that determine the environmental effects of subsidy removal**

| Main item | Item | Crucial factors | Remarks |
|---|---|---|---|
| **Step 1. Policy filter** | | | |
| Effective policy measures that reduce emissions or rates of extraction | Tradeable pollution or extraction quota. | The size of the quota after subsidy removal; Clear definition and strict enforcement. | Removal of a subsidy to the industry may have a limited or no environmental effect, if the quota *was* and remains the limiting factor after the subsidies have been removed. (The prices of quota will drop which has varying effects, *e.g.* depending on being product quota or pollution quota). However, the environmental effects remain the ones associated with the number of quotas issued). |
| Effective policy measures that reduce emissions or rates of extraction. | Tradeable pollution or extraction quota. | The size of the quota after subsidy removal. Clear definition and strict enforcement. | Removal of a subsidy to the industry may have a limited or no environmental effect, if the quota was and remains the limiting factor after the subsidies have been removed. (The prices of quota will drop which has varying effects (*e.g.* depending on being product quota or pollution quota). However the environmental effects remain the ones associated with the number of quotas issued). |
| | Production or extraction limits. | The levels of the limits. Clear definition and strict enforcement. | Subsidy removal may have a limited or no effect, if the quota was and remains the limiting factor after the subsidies have been removed. |
| | Emission standards. | The level of standards. Clear definition and strict enforcement. | Ancillary benefits by means of reductions in other emissions may not occur if they are already (sufficiently) restricted by regulation. |
| | Environmentally based taxes, charges or fees. | Rates of taxation Demand and supply elasticities of the taxed item. | Maintaining such taxes may reduce the effect of subsidy removal. |

| Main item | Item | Crucial factors | Remarks |
|---|---|---|---|
| Other limitations to production or use. | Shortfall in infrastructure. | Size of the shortfall<br>Options for expanding infrastructure.<br>Costs of the expansion.<br>Time needed for expansion of infrastructure. | Subsidy removal may have a limited or no effect, if the available infrastructure was and remains the limiting factor after the subsidies have been removed. |
| | Shortfall in other limiting factors of production: i.e. qualified labour, space. | Options for expanding the supply of the limiting factors<br>Cost of the increase in supply of the limiting factors<br>Time needed for expansion of supply of the limiting factors. | Subsidy removal may have a limited or no effect, if the limiting factors of production continue to pose limitations to production after the subsidies have been removed. (Note that the resulting high prices of the limiting factors may trigger additional supply of those limiting factors, if possible). |

*Step 2. Availability of environmentally more benign alternatives: identifying lock-in effects*

| Main item | Item | Crucial factors | Remarks |
|---|---|---|---|
| Alternative products | What competing products would benefit form the subsidy removal | Environmental profile of the subsidised product.<br>Environmental profile of the readily available competing products that would benefit from the subsidy removal.<br>Probable environmental profile of emerging alternative products.<br>Time span the subsidy has been in place. | Removing subsidies opens the way to the development of more environmentally benign alternatives. Long-standing subsidies are likely to be the most damaging. Enhancing the effectiveness of environmental policy (financial and no-financial instruments) with respect to emerging technologies may be needed to reap the benefits of technical change. |

169

| Main item | Item | Crucial factors | Remarks |
|---|---|---|---|
| **Alternative modes of production** | What modes of production would benefit from the subsidy removal. | Environmental profile of the subsidised mode of production. Environmental profile of readily available alternatives. Probable environmental profiles of emerging alternatives. Time span the subsidy has been in place. Points of impact of the subsidy. | |
| *Step 3. Higher volumes due to size, duration and conditionality of the subsidy* | | | |
| Size of the subsidy | Monetary value of the financial subsidy relative to turnover. | Elasticities of supply and demand. | Market price support can be expressed in terms of monetary value. |
| **Duration of the subsidy** | Number of years the subsidy is in place. | Technological development in competing products or modes of production outside the subsidised sector. | The longer the subsidy is in place, the stronger its lock-in effect is likely to be, thus the larger the potential environmental gains if the subsidy were to be removed. |
| *Conditionality* | | | |
| *Variable costs* | Specified energy supplies and materials | The quantitative effect of the subsidy removal on variable cost | "Materials" include (irrigation) water. Removing energy and materials subsidies shift the industries' supply curve upward and therefore immediately reduce supply at all levels of demand of the (finished) product. It will also reduce entries and eliminate lock-in effects. The environmentally beneficial effects of the reduction in production of the (finished) good may be diminished if other suppliers step in at prices only slightly above the (previously) subsidised supplies, especially if their environmental profiles are less benign. |

| Main item | Item | Crucial factors | Remarks |
|---|---|---|---|
| | Specified short lived equipment. | The quantitative effects of the subsidy removal on variable costs. Effects on the environment of the deployment of alternative types of short lived equipment. | Removing these subsidies has the same effects as removing subsidies to energy supplies and materials. If, however they have been conditional on energy or materials saving characteristics, the effect will be ambiguous. |
| *Fixed costs* | Specified types of fixed capital. Specified types of fixed capital that allow for the use of low cost, environmentally damaging inputs. Specified types of fixed capital that require the use of a particular environmentally relevant input. | The quantitative effect of the subsidy removal: — on fixed costs — on variable costs (if applicable) The (negative) effect of the subsidy removal on entries. | Removing subsidies to fixed capital reduces the profitability of the subsidised sector and will discourage entries. However if the profitability of the subsidised sector remained low, while subsidised, the effect of the subsidy removal on entries would be small or negligible. Often the choice for a particular type of fixed capital also implies certain inputs to be used. In some cases capital subsidies may allow for using cheaper inputs, thereby changing variable costs. Removing such subsidies (to fixed costs) eliminate possibly strong lock-in effects. |
| *Total costs* | Royalty concessions. | The quantitative effect of the subsidy removal — on fixed costs — on variable costs (where applicable). Environmental profiles of the subsidised activities and their alternatives. | Adjusting royalty concessions to their market value will reduce future demand for these royalties When adjusting royalties to their market price involves concessions for extraction, a strong effect may be expected on rates of depletion Since this removal may result in higher prices for inputs for downstream activities, variable costs of these downstream activities may be lowered with strong volume effects. |

| Main item | Item | Crucial factors | Remarks |
|---|---|---|---|
| *Total costs* (*continued*) | Low interest loans. | The quantitative effect of the subsidy removal<br>— on fixed costs<br>— on variable costs (where applicable).<br>Environmental profiles of the subsidised activities and their alternatives. | If low interest loans are used to reduce the costs of fixed capital, removing such subsidies will have the same effects as removing other subsidies to fixed costs<br>If granted to incumbents as well as newcomers, there will be no barriers to entry created.<br>Dependent on the relative profitability of the sector, this may lead to effects on production volumes |
| | Research and development. | The size of the subsidy relative to total operating costs.<br>Effects of the removal of the R&D subsidy on:<br>— on fixed costs<br>—on variable costs.<br>Effects of the removal of the subsidy on diminishing the environmental profile of the subsidised activity. | If the removed subsidy was large compared to operating costs, it would have been a subsidy to operating costs in disguise.<br>If the subsidy removal would imply less technical progress towards more environmentally benign technologies, the ultimate environmental effects of subsidy removal is ambiguous. |

| Main item | Item | Crucial factors | Remarks |
|---|---|---|---|
| *Profit and income* | Preferential rates of taxation. | The effect of the subsidy removal on profitability. | Decreased profitability due to the subsidy removal will discourage entries, but if entries had already been discouraged because of low profitability of the sector while subsidised, the effects on entries will be small, if not negligible., |
| | Debt write offs. | The profitability of the sector while subsidised. | When the sector produces energy and materials, downstream effects of removing the subsidy may be strong depending on the offer prices of the competitors. |
| | | The environmental profiles of the subsidised and the alternative competing economic activities. | |
| | | The environmental profiles of up-stream and down-stream economic activities. | |
| | Insufficient provision for future environmental liabilities | The nature of environmental liabilities. | Imposing sufficient provision for liabilities can render entire industries unprofitable. The environmental effects of the subsidy removal depends on the environmental profiles of the alternatives that will replace the previously subsidised sector |
| | | The effect of imposing sufficient provision of future liabilities on variable and fixed costs by means of changing modes of production, or adequate insurance. | Strong effects on downstream sectors may be expected if the previously subsidised sector supplies energy or materials, dependent on the offer prices of competing energy supplies and materials. |
| | | The environmental profiles of up-stream and down-stream economic activities. | |
| | | The environmental profiles of the (previously) subsidised sector and its competing alternatives. | |

| Main item | Item | Crucial factors | Remarks |
|---|---|---|---|
| | Exemptions from (environmental) standards). | The quantitative effect of removing the subsidy on profitability and variable and fixed costs. The effect of reduced profitability on the production volume of the sector. The environmental profiles of up-stream and down-stream economic activities. | Removing these exemptions obviously benefit the environment immediately through reducing the emissions or input use of the previously subsidised industries. Moreover the volume effects on production volumes in up-stream and down-stream industries will benefit the environment. |
| | Low rates of return requirements. | The effect of removing the low rates of return requirements on the internal discount rate of the firms. | Higher internal discount rates favour shorter-lived investments. As a result, new technologies will be deployed more rapidly (and reduce the lock-in effect). If environmental policy ensures that those new technologies are more environmentally benign, reducing the lock-in effect will benefit the environment. |

| Main item | Item | Crucial factors | Remarks |
|---|---|---|---|
| **Demand** | Low rates of VAT. Marketing promotion by governments | The tax differential relative to sales prices. The effects of marketing promotion on sales volumes. The price elasticities of demand and supply. | Demand will decrease because of subsidy removal. Its effect on production and input volumes depend on the relevant price elasticities. In the long run, the supply curve of the entire industry will be influenced by the occurrence of external effects and barriers to entry. |
| | Provision of infrastructure below cost. | The quantitative effect of internalising the cost of infrastructure on demand. The price elasticity of supply. Geographical "hot spots" where infrastructure fall short or the use of infrastructure cause high emission levels or congestion or both. The environmental profiles of the products that use that particular infrastructure. | In the long run, the supply curves of the industries that have benefited form the provision of infrastructure below costs (e.g. transport firms and those industries whose products are shipped) will be influenced by the occurrence of external effects and barriers to entry. Introducing full payment for infrastructure can increase exits from the industry. Possibly, the decrease in demand will not be sufficient to eliminate congestion or other signs of shortfall of infrastructure; thereby reducing the environmental benefits. |

*Step 4. Market power*

| Main item | Item | Crucial factors | Remarks |
|---|---|---|---|
| Market power | Market power on factor and finished goods markets | Degree of concentration. | If the previously subsidised sectors face suppliers or customers or both that wield much market power, the outcomes of removing any type of subsidy will be hard to predict. Ancillary measures are probably needed. |

# NOTES

1.  For reasons of simplicity we focus on subsidy *removal* only, and not subsidy *reform*. Subsidy reform is seen to be a combination of removing elements of a subsidy package and replacing those elements with other that have a more favourable environmental profile. A checklist that indicates subsidies for which removal benefits the environment, would facilitate both, pinpointing subsidy elements that should be removed on environmental grounds and avoiding replacing them with subsidy element that could cause environmental harm.

2.  So far subsidy removal is most often based on the negative impacts they have on the efficiency of markets (providing marketable goods and services at lowest costs). Few if any have been removed solely for environmental reasons. If subsidies were to be removed on the basis of environmental considerations, the criterion becomes a broader welfare concept that besides the efficiency of markets, also includes the efficiency of government policies in providing non-marketable goods and services.

3.  Note that these requirements include, materials and energy used in "cleaning" during the production process or afterwards.

4.  There is a strong similarity with permitting policies. Permit requirements that prescribe a certain technology are less dynamic efficient than permit requirements that stipulate environmental performance.

5.  The lock-in effect means that a certain technology simply by being applied (widely) has a competitive advantage over other (new) technologies. The lock-in effect plays a role in the path dependency of technical change.

6.  Consider for example a subsidy to energy that is used to pump irrigation water. If that subsidy is removed the costs of irrigation water rises immediately. If the acquisition price of the pump had been reduced by a subsidy, removing that subsidy would not alter the sunk costs of the pump and therefore would not raise the costs of irrigation water. The existing irrigation practices will only reduce once the pumps in use are scrapped.

176

7.      Note that removing market price support will decrease the price of the previously subsidised goods. Nevertheless, such removal will spur the development and deployment of novel technologies, since market price support must be accompanied by measures to ensure production levels above market equilibrium.

8.      The latter include "existence subsidies" that are independent of production;

9.      All subsidies that distort trade lead to a geographical relocation of environmental impacts. This means that the environment within the country that removes its subsidy could be put under more or less strain. Likewise the "world environment" could be better or worse off. The checklist allows for identifying such developments, if applied to include all the relevant sites of production.

## *Annex* 1.

## Selected Case Studies

## Introduction

Unfortunately, quantitative assessments of the effects subsidies vary over extremely wide ranges, even if they apply to the same sort of subsidies (see, for example, OECD, 1997a, b, c and d). This is partly due to differences between *definitions* of a subsidy and the comprehensiveness of the *policy package (policy design* of the particular subsidy) under study. Other explanations are the *circumstances* under which the subsidies are applied, the differences between the models (*e.g.* top-down or bottom-up),[1] and the economic and technical assumptions which underlie the calculations. Often the differences between the assumed alternative technology or economic activity that will emerge when the subsidy is removed (the benchmark) has a strong effect on the outcomes of the analyses (see, for example, OECD, 1997a). Looking at numerous case studies, however, reveals factors that seem to be important in many analyses.[2] The simplified and by no means comprehensive descriptions that follow in the next paragraphs only serve to highlight the various ways subsidies may affect volumes produced and consumed. It is selective, including only those elements that the author thinks have a strong bearing on the environmental effects of subsidy removal. These elements are elaborated upon in the main body of the paper.

---

1.      Top-down models are based on the usual demand and supply functions. Bottom-up models start from descriptions of technological alternatives and use an algorithm to calculate optimal solutions.

2.      Reviewing all available case studies is beyond the present scope. The reader is referred to review studies, such as Porter (2003).

## Agriculture

Few areas, if any, have been studied in more detail than agricultural subsidies. The OECD's work on the "Policy Evaluation Matrix", based on transfer efficiency formulas, and using a vast amount of available statistical data, has revealed the remarkable differences between the effects of various types of subsidies (basically: deficiency payments, market price support, subsidies to acreage, subsidies to other inputs) on the incidence and transfer efficiency of agricultural subsidies (see, for example, OECD, 2001b). This leads to an important conclusion regarding the economic characteristics that make subsidies environmentally harmful. A very large portion of support leaks away to input suppliers, non-farming landowners and other sectors of the economy and leads to significant upstream changes in production volumes. In addition, subsidies that lead to lower agricultural prices are implicit subsidies to the food processing industries. Studying the total environmental effects of subsidies to agriculture therefore must involve the supplying sectors. Another conclusion would be that these subsidies, while not efficient in improving farmers' incomes lead to more production, if not restricted by other measures or circumstances.

Although there are several studies indicating that production and input subsidies lead to more intensive farming practices (Porter, 2003), there are few studies that investigate the effects of subsidy removal. Rainelli (1998) argues that replacing a subsidy to irrigation water by a subsidy on historical revenues will not reduce the use of irrigation water, since the new subsidy will not decrease the prices of land, therefore continuing to contain an incentive to intensive farming. However, the need for irrigation water might be reduced as investments to increase the efficiency of irrigation become more profitable). After all, the mode of production chosen by the farmer depends on the relative prices of factors of production.

A recent study for the Netherlands (Massink and Meester, 2002), based on comparing several policy scenarios of which one is a recourse to free trade, indicates that total subsidy removal would lead to significant income transfers, changes in the composition of Dutch agricultural production and, relevant to the present subject, a further intensification of agriculture.[3]

Apparently, neither changing subsidy regimes nor abolishing subsidies altogether automatically will reverse the incentive towards intensification that has resulted from agricultural policies that included the subsidies. This

---

3.   The environmental effects of increased intensification are probably ambiguous, since larger areas may become available for less environmentally damaging uses.

asymmetry between introducing and removing subsidies, necessitates closely examination of the "economics on the farm level" and more precisely defining the all the relevant policy changes made.

## Energy: electricity and coal

The OECD report on *Reforming energy and Transport Subsidies: Environmental and Economic Implications* (OECD, 1997) includes two large case studies regarding on the benefits of removing subsidies that lead to different conclusions.

DRI (1997), studying the impacts of phasing out coal subsidies in OECD countries using the PSE definition of subsidies and applying a top-down trade model structure, found small environmental effects. Phasing out coal subsidies (of the market price support type) would mainly result in using imported coal in stead of domestically produced (and subsidised) coal. According to this study due to the economics of fuel use, coal would remain the preferred fuel for electricity generation, both in the short and long run.

By contrast, Naughten *et al.* (1997), use a bottom-up (linear programming) model for Australia, based on a database of technologies and defining subsidies as the difference between the minimum cost of an optimal combination of technologies that satisfy a certain level of electricity demand, on the one hand, and the costs of policy-determined alternatives on the other, analysed the effects of various elements of energy policies. These policy elements include a deliberate choice for a certain fuel (coal) for a newly built power plant, capital subsidies and trade distortions. For each of such policy elements, the subsidy is defined as the wedge it creates with the least-cost solution for generating the demanded electricity.

They find that removing subsidies that are implicit in energy policy — notably loan guarantees, provision of loans at below market rates to (government-owned) coal-fired power stations and trade restrictions between Australian states that prevailed before regulatory reform — would result in a significant fuel shift towards combined cycle gas turbine (CCGT) electricity generation. This result is based on the higher capital intensity of coal-fired electricity generation, shorter lead times in building a CCGT-plant compared to a coal-fired plant, as well as the more modular character of CCGT generation which makes it more economical if production has to respond to changes in demand. Removing the subsidies to capital and privatising power plants, would result in higher rate-of-return requirements (from 8% to an assumed 15%) and therefore would result in a shift to gas, even if coal would remain the cheapest fuel per Kwh, if power plants are designed according to their technical optimal size.

It is important to realise that subsidies to energy producers and energy products (such as low preferential tax rates) will be (at least partially) passed on to industries and households. Removing them will affect downstream emissions.

## Irrigation water

Removing subsidies to irrigation water generally can have two distinct effects: agriculture on previously irrigated land would cease to be profitable if not becoming entirely impossible, or lead to inefficient use of water, or both. Increased efficiency, of course, can mitigate the effect on profitability. Most studies have focused on optimal pricing of water using either the yardstick of full-cost recovery or the marginal value product of the water, which equals the value of the incremental volume of production due to the use of one unit of water.

Little is known about the environmental effects of removing water subsidies (by whatever definition), and what information is available is difficult to generalise because of the country and site specificity of the institutional arrangements, the multiple uses served by water infrastructure and environmental conditions. Presumably the following conclusion could be drawn. Both the feasibility to arrive at water pricing systems that reflect more the costs of water or its marginal productivity and its environmental effects is strongly interwoven with other policies and comprehensive water management systems. As is stated in OECD (1999b), referring to Australian experiences, "water pricing reforms must be accompanied by other important mechanisms, in absence of which pure pricing mechanisms might yield few benefits."

Existing infrastructure represents sunk cost. Removing subsidies that consists of users not paying in full for that infrastructure shifts the financial burden from the taxpayer to the consumer, which may lead to firms leaving the industry. If that leads to a reduction in demand, under-utilisation of existing infrastructure may arise. The "optimal" price structure when subsides are removed, therefore may differ from the "optimal" price structure if no subsidies had been granted. Secondly the environmental effects of the waterworks do not disappear when the subsidies are removed.

## Transport

In the transport sector much attention have been paid to the social costs of transport (such as pollution, accidents, congestion). Not internalising these marginal social costs have been labelled by some as (implicit) subsidies. Apart from subsidies arising from any incomplete internalisation of these social costs, very substantial subsidies are the result of non-internalisation of the costs of infrastructure. The costs of infrastructure is particularly relevant because of the high ratios of fixed to variable costs and high sunk costs (Porter, 2003).

As a result, much recent work concerning subsidy removal (*e.g.* Roy, 2000) boils down to removing the inequalities in the treatment of the cost of infrastructure, although other elements such as preferential low tax rates on particular fuels and tolls may cause distortions in variable costs as well. Generally there is over-pricing and under-utilisation of rail and under-pricing and over-utilisation of roads.

The ways subsidies to infrastructure lead to higher transport volumes, transport-related pollution and congestion is quite complex. This can be illustrated by a simplified example.[4] If, for example, a road between points A and B is constructed or improved, transport costs (and time) between the two points is reduced. Moreover, demand for road transport between A and B increases, either because a latent demand is activated (a shift along the original demand curve) or because the lower costs of transportation by road attracts transport demand that previously was satisfied by other modes of transportation (a shift of the demand curve itself). If road transport does not pay for the improvement of this road infrastructure, a new subsidy is created that increases demand. Quite possibly this higher level of demand leads to more congestion on the road between A and B, but also on other roads leading to A or B which in turn will lengthen the travel time, and hence costs, between A and B as well as to A or B. This will be accentuated if at the same time, there exists subsidies to particular road users, such as preferential tax rates on fuel, capital or labour.

The environmental effects of subsidies to various modes of transport consist of two distinct categories: the effects on transport volumes and the effects on the level and geographical distribution of economic activities. Studies reveal that the price elasticities of demand for transport strongly depend on the availability of alternative modes of transport and other route dependent factors. Estimating the environmental benefits of changes in the price structure of transport therefore, require rather detailed modelling. The other environmental

---

4.      See for example the description of the TRENEN model in Roy (2000).

effects of removing subsidies to transport, those related to the level and geographical distribution of industrial emissions, are even harder to predict. Needless to say that they can have significant effects on local environments.

**Fisheries**

Hanneson (2001) points to the importance of management regimes on the effects of subsidy removal on fish stocks. He distinguishes three such regimes: (1) *open access*, where there is no control over the quantity of catches nor over fishing effort. It is probably no longer very representative for OECD countries; (2) *catch control*, where the total amount caught is regulated; and (3) *effective management*, under which the amount of catches is set at an economically optimal level and the costs to catch this amount are minimised, for example by means of individual transferable quotas. If the total amount of allowed catch is perfectly enforced (a big "if"), subsidy removal will not lead to less catches under the catch control or effective management regime, provided that the regime imposes limits on the catches below the level that would occur after the withdrawal of the subsidy. Under open access, by contrast, removing cost-reducing subsidies could very well lead to new entrants and continued over-fishing. In all these cases, removing cost-reducing subsidies have little effect, if at all.

As is true in most sectors, subsidies come in a wide variety (WWF, 2001) and the responses of fishermen to these various types of subsidies may differ strongly. Subsidies to fuel, for example, immediately affect the cost of each trip and deprive more energy-efficient propulsion and refrigeration from some, if not all, its cost advantage. Removing them is likely to have an immediate effect. Removing subsidies that affect the costs of the vessel, by contrast, will primarily reduce the entrance of new vessels. Fishing port infrastructure is likely to open up or enlarge markets with no costs for the fishermen, stimulating demand and supply, and removing them can make fishermen leaving the sector. Foreign access payments by governments enlarge their fishing grounds at no cost to the fishermen. Substantial subsidies are paid for alleviating the hardships of restructuring the fishing industry. Although they may not be as effective as desirable, removing them could make reducing capacity politically even more difficult as it is. Holland *et al.* (1999) highlight the importance of differences in design and other circumstances for the effectiveness of fishing vessel buy back schemes. This sounds as a warning that policy design and circumstances might be decisive for the effectiveness of other removals of subsidies.

183

## Annex 2.

## The Role of Elasticities

Subsidies leak away from their intended recipients. Suppliers will raise their prices in view of increased demand and customers will pay less if supply is increased. When subsidies are removes, generally, the opposite will occur. The degree in which this happens depends on the price elasticities of both supply and demand for the final product of the subsidised sector. In Figure A2.a and b the role of price elasticities, as well as the effect of forward linkage is illustrated.

Assume no substitution between inputs (not change of technology). Then the decrease in sales of the final product equals the decrease in input sales. The total environmental burden then decreases with the sum of $\Delta E_f$ and $\Delta E_i$. If the production of the input has a larger environmental burden per unit of output which is often the case, then the larger portion of the environmental improvement caused by the reduction in the demand for the input.

$\Delta Q_{f \text{ and } i}$ depends on the size of the subsidy and the elasticities of supply and demand of the final product as follows:

In panel a, let $\beta_f$ be the price increase due to the loss of the subsidy U, and $\gamma_f$ be the relative volume decrease related to the relative price increase in terms of the withdrawn subsidy U.

$$\beta_f = \frac{\Delta P_{f1}}{U} \text{ ; and } \qquad \gamma_f = \frac{\Delta Q_f / Q_{f1}}{U / P_{f1}}$$

The price elasticities of demand and supply (absolute value) are:

$$\eta_f^d = \frac{\Delta Q_f}{\Delta P_f} * \frac{P_{f1}}{Q_{f1}} \text{ ; and } \qquad \eta_f^s = \frac{\Delta Q_f}{U - \Delta P_f} * \frac{P_{f1}}{Q_{f1}}$$

Then:

$$\beta_f = \frac{\eta_f^s}{\eta_f^s + \eta_f^d} \text{ ; and } \qquad \gamma_f = \eta_f^d * \beta_f$$

184

# Figure A2. Quantity responses of suppliers due to subsidy removal

**Panel a: input subsidies; final product**     **Panel b: quantity response: suppliers**

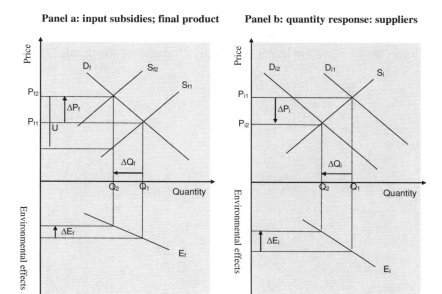

## Key

| | | | |
|---|---|---|---|
| D: | Demand curve | P: | Price |
| S: | Supply curve | Q: | Quantity |
| E | Environmental effect curve   U | Subsidy | |

Suffix 1, 2: With and without a subsidy respectively
Suffix f, i: Final product, input respectively
$\Delta Q_f$, $\Delta Q_i$: Quantity decrease in the sales of the final product and the input respectively

In Panel b, the relative price increase of the input is

$$\frac{\Delta P_i}{P_{i1}} = \frac{1}{\eta_i^s} * \frac{\Delta Q_i}{Q_{i1}} = \frac{1}{\eta_i^s} * \frac{\Delta Q_f}{\Delta Q_{i1}}$$

This is a very simplified model. In reality, the weighted average of the supply elasticities of the inputs equals the supply elasticity of the final product. This (over) simplified model, nevertheless, illustrates the role of the demand and supply elasticities in determining the effects of the removal of a subsidy that lowers marginal production costs. The quantitative relationships between subsidy removal and volume effects can only be established using partial or, preferably, general equilibrium models.

The conclusion remains that the removal of a cost reducing subsidy might have significant upstream environmental effects. All other things being equal, this is the more so the larger the supply elasticity of the input.

# REFERENCES

Ayres, Robert U. and Leslie W. Ayres, with contributions by Paolo Frankl, Howard Lee, Paul M. Weaver, Nicole Wolfgang (1996), *Industrial Ecology: Towards Closing the Materials Cycle*, Edward Elgar, Cheltenham, UK and Brookfield, US.

Burniaux, J.-M., J. Martin and J. Oliveira-Martins (1992), "The Effects of Existing Distortions in Energy Markets on the Cost of Policies to Reduce $CO_2$-emissions: evidence from GREEN", *OECD Economic Studies,* Winter 1992.

Chen, Duanjie (1999), "The Effects of Taxes and Support on Marginal Costs: Quantitative Illustrations", in OECD, *Improving the Environment through Reducing Subsidies: Part III, Case Studies,* OECD, Paris.

Hannesson, Rögnvaldur (2001), *Effects of Liberalizing Trade in Fishing Services and Investments in Fishing Vessels*, OECD Papers Offprint No. 8, Paris

Holland, Dan, Eyjolfur Gudmundson and John Gates (1999), "Do Fishing Vessel Buyback Programs Work: A Survey of the Evidence", *Marine Policy,* Vol. 23, No. 1, pp. 47-69.

Larsen, B. and A. Shah (1992), "World Fossil Fuel Subsidies and Global Carbon Emissions", Policy Research Working Paper Series, No. 1002, World Bank, Washington, DC.

Massink, Henk and Gerrit Meester (2002), *Boeren bij Vrijhandel: De Nederlandse Agrosector bij Handelsliberalisatie en EU-uitbreiding: Een verkenning,* Ministerie van Landbouw, Natuurbeheer en Visserij, Den Haag, (in Dutch).

Naughten, Barry, Jane Melanie and Jan Dlugosz (1997), "Modelling 'Supports' to the Electricity sector in Australia", in OECD, *Reforming Energy and Transport Subsidies: Environmental and Economic Implications,* OECD, Paris; based on "Supports to the Electricity Sector in Australia", in OECD, *Environmental Implications of Energy and Transport Subsidies, Volume 2, Support to the Coal Industry and the Electricity Sector*, Document No. OECD/GD(97)155, OECD, Paris.

OECD (1997a), *Environmental Implications of Energy and Transport Subsidies, Volume 1, Scoping Study: Greenhouse Gas Impacts of Russian Energy Subsidies, Climate Change Impacts of Subsidies to the Energy Sector in the USA,* Document No. OECD/GD(97)154, OECD, Paris.

OECD (1997b), *Environmental Implications of Energy and Transport Subsidies, Volume 2, Support to the Coal Industry and the Electricity Sector*, Document No. OECD/GD(97)155, OECD, Paris.

OECD (1997c), *Environmental Implications of Energy and Transport Subsidies, Volume 3, Support to the Road Transport Sector*, Document No. OECD/GD(97)156, OECD, Paris.

OECD (1997d), *Reforming Energy and Transport Subsidies: Environmental and Economic Implications*, OECD, Paris.

OECD (1998), *Improving the Environment through Reducing Subsidies: Part I, Summary and Policy Conclusions, Part II, Analysis and Overview of Studies*, OECD, Paris.

OECD (1999a), *Improving the Environment through Reducing Subsidies: Part III, Case Studies*, OECD, Paris.

OECD (1999b), *Agricultural Water Pricing in OECD countries*, Environment Directorate, Working Party on Economic and Environmental Policy Integration, ENV/EPOC/GEEI(98)11/FINAL, Paris

Pillet, Gonzague, (1999), "Effective Tax Rates on Marginal Costs of Different Modes of Freight Transport", in OECD, *Improving the Environment through Reducing Subsidies: Part III, Case Studies*, OECD, Paris.

Porter, Gareth (2003), "Subsidies and the Environment: An Overview of the State of Knowledge", paper prepared for the OECD Workshop on Environmentally Harmful Subsidies, Paris, 7-8 November, published in this volume.

Roy, Rana (ed.) (2000), *Revenues from Efficient Pricing: Evidence from the Member States*, UIC/CER/European Commission DG-TREN Study, London

Steenblik, Ronald P. and P. Coryannakis (1995), "Reform of Coal Policies in Western and Central Europe: Implications for the Environment", *Energy Policy*, Vol. 23, No 6, pp. 537-553.

World Wildlife Fund (2001), *Hard Facts, Hidden Problems: A Review of Current Data on Fishing Subsidies*, WWF Technical Paper, Gland, Switzerland, http://www.worldwildlife.org/oceans/hard_facts.pdf.

# SUMMARY AND CONCLUSIONS

*by*
*Michel POTIER*
*Consultant, France*

This Workshop provided the first forum in which experts from a variety of backgrounds (government, academics, researchers and representatives of international organisations and civil society) could gather together in an international forum to take stock of the technical knowledge of subsidies and their environmental impacts in such diverse areas as agriculture, fisheries, energy, industry, transport, forestry and water resources.

Is it possible to agree on a common definition of a subsidy and on methods to measure them? How can the environmental impact of a subsidy, or group of subsidies, be detected and measured? Is there any correlation between the scope or size of subsidies and their harmful impact on the environment? Are enough reliable data and methods available to identify, measure and analyse environmentally harmful subsidies? Such were the main questions that the participants tried to answer.

The Workshop's conclusions can be summarised in four major categories:

- context, synergies and tradeoffs;
- conceptual differences and foundations;
- empirical data on subsidies and their impact on the environment; and
- possible directions for future OECD work.

## Context, synergies and tradeoffs

The Workshop agreed that the debate over environmentally harmful subsidies should be placed in the broader context of sustainable development. That entails weighing up the overall environmental impacts of subsidies with their economic and social effects. Measuring the costs and benefits of multiple

189

government interventions would be a challenging exercise, but one which could significantly assist in framing the issues and generating appropriate questions.

From the standpoint of sustainable development, subsidies are potentially harmful if they adversely affect one or more of the stocks of capital (natural capital, produced capital, human capital and social capital) that contribute to the well-being of humankind. Concrete examples would be subsidies that impede desirable technological change or deepen poverty. Expanding the analysis to encompass the effects of subsidies on human and social capital would be a major step, because the linkages between subsidies and the formation of social and human capital are generally of an indirect nature. Similarly, the importance of technological progress should not be underestimated. And, given that the poor carry much of the burden of protectionist policies, it is also necessary to explore how subsidies affect poverty in both developed and developing countries.

Much emphasis was placed on the need to look not only at the *direct effects* of subsidies on natural capital, but also at their *indirect effects*. By "direct effect" is meant the impact that a subsidy has on the environment as a result of induced changes in levels or patterns of production or consumption. "Indirect effects" occur in more subtle ways. The persistence of poverty, for example, can force people to have to choose short-term degradation of their local environment – even thought they know it could undermine the natural capital on which their future welfare depends – just to be able to survive. Deterioration of the environment can also cause the erosion of social capital through loss of community, decline in trust or increased corruption. The measurement of such indirect effects runs up against many difficulties, but should nevertheless constitute an avenue of research for the future.

The Workshop participants agreed that there are significant synergies to be gained from examining the issue of environmentally harmful subsidies, both across sectors and within the sustainable development framework. One of the main aims of the Workshop was to pool experiences and knowledge from the various sectors, and it was clear that there is much to gain from such information sharing. This is especially so given that the various sectors are at different stages in their identification and analysis of subsidies. The sustainable development framework also provides a broader perspective with which to exploit available synergies.

The issue of tradeoffs emerged as a consistent theme in the Workshop in two contexts. First, the broad definition of sustainable development implies that there may often need to be some tradeoffs among the various forms of capital that make up the total stock of capital available to humankind. While it is desirable to pursue "win-win" outcomes, they may not always be achievable. Second, it was reinforced that the optimal level of pollution resulting from economic activity is not generally zero. As a result, a cautionary note is required: reform or removal of environmentally harmful subsidies will not by itself solve environmental problems, but such steps are a necessary part of the process of improving environmental outcomes.

## Conceptual differences and foundations

### *Defining subsidies*

In general terms, the Workshop concluded that the elements of a common definition and framework for subsidies currently exist, although there remains the challenging task of providing a formal, unifying framework. In general, a subsidy is a result of government action that confers an advantage on consumers or producers, in order to supplement their income or lower their costs. This broad definition, or significant elements of it, can be found in the analysis of subsidies across the sectors examined at the Workshop. The terminology that has been used has varied between sectors depending on, among other things, the purpose for which the particular subsidy was adopted. For example, depending on circumstances, subsidies are variously referred to as transfers, payments, support, assistance or aid. Workshop attendees agreed that adoption of a more common rhetoric would help minimise confusion when comparing information from different sectors.

The WTO definition of a subsidy was recognised as being a useful starting point for the analysis of subsidies. It is the only internationally agreed definition of a subsidy and contains most of the elements of the broader definition used by the OECD (with two key exceptions: government-provided general infrastructure and price support). Organising frameworks that can be used to build on the WTO definition to better define and measure subsidies include the effective rate of assistance concept and the existing system of national accounts. A cautionary note was offered on using the term "implicit subsidy". This has been increasingly used to refer to the monetised value of (negative) externalities generated by an activity and goes beyond the meaning generally ascribed to a subsidy.

In terms of defining what constitutes an environmentally harmful subsidy, the Workshop concluded that the definition adopted by the OECD in its earlier study on reducing environmentally harmful subsidies is a good starting point: "a subsidy can be defined as 'environmentally harmful' if it encourages more environmental damage to take place than what would occur without the subsidy" (OECD, 1998). Achieving consensus on measuring techniques and

191

methods seems to be the most promising avenue, provided there is greater transparency in classifying the information.

## *Measuring subsidies*

The stocktaking of OECD work on subsidies to date has identified five main approaches to measuring them, some of which overlap:

- Programme aggregation: adding up the budgetary transfers of relevant government programmes; in most cases data are at the national, and not sub-national level.

- Price-gap: measuring the difference between the world and domestic market prices of the product in question.

- Producer/consumer support estimate: measuring the budgetary transfers and price gaps under relevant government programmes affecting production and consumption alike.

- Resource rent: measuring the resource rent foregone for natural resources.

- Marginal social cost: measuring the difference between the price actually charged and the marginal social cost.

An OECD paper presented at the Workshop reviews subsidy definitions and coverage in six sectors of the economy (agriculture, fisheries, forestry, energy, manufacturing and transport), along with irrigation water (Honkatukia, 2002). It is clear that there are differences across the sectors:

- *Agriculture*: the most commonly used definitions and measures of subsidies are the producer support estimate (PSE), the consumer support estimate (CSE), the total support estimate (TSE), calculated annually by the OECD; and the aggregate measurement of support (AMS) used in the GATT Uruguay Round and WTO agricultural negotiations. OECD estimates cover market price support, financial transfers (including those to reduce the cost of fixed capital and/or variable inputs), general services (transfers covering the costs of research, marketing and structural/infrastructure services) and consumption subsidies. Data are available with respect to both production and consumption.

- *Fisheries*: the OECD measures transfers to reduce the costs of fixed capital and/or variable inputs; direct payments; general services (transfers covering the costs of research,

192

management, and enforcement and infrastructure); and, to some extent, price support through market measures.

- *Energy*: the OECD measures grants or soft loans to producers or consumers of energy; market price support; differential tax rates on different fuels; and publicly funded research and development programmes. Data are available with respect to production in the case of coal subsidies.

- *Transport*: subsidies are commonly measured on a purely financial basis as the gap between government expenditures on transport systems and the revenues collected from those systems. Measurement on an economic basis has also been attempted, on the basis of the deficit or surplus of revenues produced by current taxes and charges compared with those that would pertain in an optimum where all transport services are priced at their marginal social costs (including the external costs of congestion, scarcity, accidents, noise, air pollution, climate change and so on).

- *Manufacturing*: measured subsidies include grants and interest rate subsidies, tax exemptions, soft loans, equity investments, tax deferrals and loan guarantees.

- Irrigation water: subsidies are measured either as government expenditure covering all or some of the costs of installing and/or maintaining irrigation systems, or on the basis of the water's true value to the irrigator.

The Workshop emphasised the need to:

- consider all types of policy intervention, including budget and off-budget transfers;

- distinguish between transfers and non-internalised externalities; and

- make the presentation of subsidy accounts more transparent.

It would also be better to avoid using the term "subsidy", but rather to speak of "support", which is a more neutral term and covers a wider range of transfers (including those for goods and services for which markets are missing).

Ideally, the classification system should be multidimensional, containing information about the *mechanisms* for granting support (basis for implementation); *targets* of that support (intended beneficiaries, such as producers or consumers); and *policy context* (public priorities and objectives). It should be designed in such a way that data can be organised to produce aggregates for any category of subsidy.

When subsidies are accompanied by regulatory measures to limit inputs, production, depletion of natural resources or damage to the environment, such information should be compiled to assess the environmental *impact* of subsidies, and this dimension should be added to the classification of subsidies. This approach results in two-dimensional matrices with "types of subsidies" constituting one dimension, and "production constraints (conditionality) or management regime" the other. This matrix approach is being used for the agriculture sector and has been used in fisheries. It was stressed that it would be useful to test whether the approach could be taken in other sectors as well.

### Environmentally harmful subsidies

Discussion at the Workshop showed the difficulty of distinguishing subsidies that were potentially harmful from those that had no impact, or a beneficial impact, on the environment, as well as the complexity of the relationships between the elimination of a subsidy and its environmental impact. There is not, in fact, a "one-to-one" linkage between the magnitude or type of support in a given sector, and the damage inflicted on the environment. Equally, there is no direct linkage between the elimination of a subsidy and improvement to the environment.

The environmental impact of a support measure depends on a number of characteristics determined by the way in which a given level of support is provided, and the nature of the:

- markets for intermediate and finished products;
- available replacement technologies, products or services causing less environmental stress;
- tax system in force;
- regulatory and institutional framework; and
- local biophysical features of the receiving environment.

To take into account these features and to be able to identify subsidies whose removal would be beneficial for the environment, the Workshop proposed to use a checklist. The checklist is based on the nature of the conditions for support and certain context-specific information.

The checklist classifies the various support measures according to the transfers generated and the method of implementation (market price support, support for inputs, direct income support). A two-dimensional matrix could show the magnitude or size of subsidies on one side and how they are implemented on the other. The Workshop suggested that the checklist could be widened, such as by adding a criterion relating to the political impediments to subsidy reform.

The checklist also raises a series of questions. To what extent do other regulations in place limit or exacerbate damage to the environment? Would the technologies and products likely to replace subsidised technologies and products cause less pollution? What would be the most probable responses of the affected industries in terms of production volume or the rate of natural resource exploitation?

Using this checklist demonstrates that, in the short-run, subsidies that reduce variable costs (such as energy and materials, including water) are more likely to impact on production (and thus emissions) than subsidies that lower fixed costs. The environmental harm of these subsidies is aggravated if they delay the development and dissemination of new technologies that increase resource productivity while cutting back on environmentally harmful effects. Other subsidies likely to have an environmentally harmful effect are those that lower the cost of access to natural resources, and capital subsidies that impede or thwart technological change, locking in potentially less efficient uses of energy and other materials.

The proposed checklist was regarded by participants as a pragmatic approach for providing policymakers with insights that could help them rank subsidies according to their degree of harmfulness to the environment. In addition, it was emphasised that it is important to consider not only the environmental impact of a given subsidy, but the impact of the entire mix of subsidies that are concurrently applied, in view of their interactions, and to examine the tax consequences of withdrawing a subsidy. Finally, the checklist could foster stronger co-operation between various governmental or non-governmental organisations through the sharing of data.

**Empirical data on subsidies and their impact on the environment**

Despite the progress that had been made, the data on subsidies currently available was found patchy across sectors and countries, and quality was variable. First, the only data available across the economy are those produced for national accounts systems, but the subsidy categories given in that framework are defined very narrowly (do not include market price support, for example) and related only to gross transfers. Second, because detailed subsidy data available relating to certain products, industries or sectors used different definitions, coverage of policies and methods of calculation and classification, it is not readily comparable. Third, since most data on subsidies have been compiled for reasons other than to analyse their potential effects on the environment, the categories into which subsidies have been aggregated might not be suitable for that purpose. Lastly, it could be difficult to match data on subsidies with information on environmental variables, insofar as data on subsidies often related to a given sector, whereas data on the environment tended to relate to specific products or technologies. In sum, these factors limit the analysis of the potential environmental impact of subsidies.

Data comparability has been achieved in some cases, as in common analytical frameworks of national accounting and the existing sectional support accounts – for example, in calculating the nominal assistance coefficient (NAC), the producer support estimate (PSE), the consumer support estimate (CSE) and the effective rate of assistance (ERA). However, narrow classifications by sector or by national territory are of limited use when countries are confronted with a range of environmental and social threats with global impacts.

### Empirical data on subsidies

#### Agriculture

This is the sector for which the most data are available. Data published annually by the OECD on the overall levels and composition of agricultural support for OECD countries, and those published by the WTO in connection with trade policy reviews, are the main sources of information available. Data for non-OECD countries and at the sub-national level are patchy for some countries.

#### Irrigation water

No organisation is currently compiling or distributing data on irrigation water subsidies in a comprehensive manner. Nevertheless, some data are gathered by the OECD, the World Bank and certain independent researchers, using one of the two definitions of irrigation water subsidies.

#### Fisheries

Data have been compiled by the OECD since 1996 and the OECD remains the only continuing systematic effort to measure subsidies to the fishing sector.

APEC, the WTO, non-governmental organisations like the WWF and independent researchers have also undertaken studies, generally of a one-off nature. Overall, there are gaps in the information gathered (especially with reference to tax relief and regional and local subsidies), making in-depth analysis of the data difficult. Market price support is not calculated explicitly, and serious gaps exist for subsidies in countries outside the OECD area.

## Forestry

There are no comparable data regarding financial transfers to the forestry sector, either for the OECD countries or for other groups of countries. In the absence of a systematic information–gathering effort, a study launched by the European Forest Institute will go some way towards filling this vacuum.

## Energy

Yearly estimates of coal support are regularly reported by the IEA, and date back to the mid-1980s. The European Commission maintains a database on public grants to collieries. But information on subsidies for other forms of energy other than coal is not collected regularly at the international level and are often highly variable. Partial information may be found in the detailed energy policy studies of the IEA Member countries, in *ad hoc* studies by the IEA, OECD, World Bank and independent researchers. Data on prices in the energy sector are also readily available for OECD countries.

## Transport

Data on public expenditures on transport infrastructure, external costs and revenue from the use of transport are available for a number of countries. The UNITE research program of the European Commission has collected data for many EU countries and provides the most comprehensive set of data available. The European Conference of Ministers of Transport (ECMT) has modelled optimal charges for the use of inland transport infrastructure in five of its member countries.

## Environmental impact of subsidies

Quantifying the environmental impact of subsidies is an analytical challenge for all of the sectors studied.

*Agriculture*

Most of the studies available analyse the linkages between support for agriculture, production and the effects on water, air and soil, particularly related to farming practices and the use of fertilisers pesticides, and greenhouse gases, but are also starting to look at other environmental effects, such as biodiversity or landscape. There are several studies on the production effects of trade liberalisation in agriculture at the global level, and some progress in the OECD on quantifying the environmental impacts in selected commodity sectors for OECD countries, as well as similar studies for non-OECD countries (FAO, UNEP). A major challenge is to specify the linkages between support, production and multiple environmental effects, which vary significantly at the regional or local level.

*Irrigation water*

Most of the existing studies make the connection between eliminating subsidies and saving water, but do not otherwise incorporate environmental variables explicitly. There is a lack of data concerning correlations of irrigation water-related environmental indicators (such as intensity of currents, nitrate levels in water, soil toxicity, groundwater levels, and loss of soil productivity due to catchment area salinity) with changes in the amounts of subsidies.

*Fisheries*

The OECD recently examined the effects of subsidies on trade. The analysis is now starting to increase understanding of the linkages between the various management regimes (open access, catch control and effective management) and subsidies, and putting them in the broader analytical framework of sustainable development.

*Forestry*

No quantitative methodologies appear to estimate the environmental impact of subsidies in the forestry sector. There are very few studies in this field, and there is a need to establish the linkage between the rate of exploitation of a forest and the level of support.

*Energy*

Most of the studies carried out in this area focus on the potential impact of eliminating subsidies on greenhouse gases, and on $CO_2$ in particular. More recent analysis in the energy sector is more focused on non-OECD countries rather than for the OECD this latter gap needs to be addressed.

*Transport*

There are many studies analysing the environmental impact of various modes of transport, but generally the studies available provide no way to measure the environmental impact of reducing a subsidy through internalisation of external costs. As mentioned earlier, the ECMT work does address this task.

*Manufacturing*

No study appears to be available that makes the connection between eliminating subsidies and the impact on the environment.

The main conclusion which emerges is that there are still formidable hurdles to overcome – specifying the relationships, gathering relevant data, and modelling the linkages. Moreover, where studies have been conducted, they limited the examination of environmental impacts to only some of the relevant variables.

**Possible directions for future OECD work**

A number of avenues for the OECD's short- or medium-term future work were raised, taking account of the Organisation's comparative advantages relative to other IGOs and NGOs. These involve the collection and dissemination of data on subsidies, work to improve the conceptual framework for understanding the linkages between subsidies and their impact on the environment (testing the proposed checklist), reinforcing co-operation between various institutions that are working on the issue, and reviewing the linkages (synergies and tradeoffs) between subsidies and sustainable development.

Practical difficulties in internalising externalities remain central among obstacles to the phasing out of harmful subsidies agreed by OECD Ministers. Overcoming this obstacle requires a coherent prescription for action in light of three distinct, but evolving contexts. First, the conditions under scrutiny – the environment – are changing as we make our observations and measurements. Second, technologies are evolving rapidly, often outpacing changes in policy development. Third, the structures and constitutions of many organisations are undergoing fundamental changes, reflecting changing public concerns and importance of different constituencies.

Development of the work and the establishment of a network of experts, as recommended by the Workshop, will not easily advance removal of obstacles to policy reform without reinforcement of a high-level mandate. Useful outcomes from a series of technical tasks and their successful implementation will continue to depend on firm political commitment.

The Workshop suggested that the OECD undertake the following areas of work.

### *Supplement existing databases on subsidies, update them regularly and distribute them more widely*

Alongside the pursuit of work on collecting data for the agriculture, fisheries, transport, energy and industrial sectors, there is a need to distribute the information gathered by OECD to a wide audience via a website. It was noted, moreover, that the creation of a centralised website serving all practitioners in the field would reduce transaction costs.

### *Improve the conceptual framework for analysing the environmental impact of subsidies and testing the checklist*

OECD is in a good position to stimulate dialogue between experts and conduct peer reviews of the methodologies used or proposed in order to assess the environmental impact of subsidies. It is in this context that the checklist discussed during the Workshop should also be tested. A key question here is whether the starting point should be the environmental impact – making a distinction between the overall and the local impact and working back to the subsidy – or vice versa, *i.e.* to start with the total amount of the subsidies and examine their overall or local impact. In some sectors it is apparent that subsidies are large (such as agriculture, irrigation water and fisheries), while in others environmental issues are significant (such as energy and transport), which suggests that both approaches seem desirable and complementary and would be partly determined by practical considerations. Nevertheless, there was general agreement at the Workshop that subsidy accounts should be designed with environmental analysis in mind, but also recognising that a range of other analytical considerations (such as economic and social impacts) remain important.

### *Strengthen co-operation between the various institutions working in this area*

It was emphasised that it would be useful for the OECD to strengthen co-operation among the various institutions known for their work on subsidies, such as the World Bank, the FAO and the WTO, but also research institutions and non-governmental organisations that are active in the field and not subject to political constraints in choosing their research programmes. It would also be desirable to set up a network of experts – modelled on that of statisticians in the area of national accounts – to exchange views and share experience and data on the better incorporation of subsidies into the system of national accounts, and on the analysis of subsidies and their environmental effects.

## *Examine the linkages between subsidies and sustainable development*

Subsidies often have an impact on more than one aspect of sustainable development – the impacts can be both positive and negative for the environmental, economic and social pillars. In order to provide a better understanding of the overall benefits and costs, tradeoffs and impacts of subsidy reform, the environmental aspects should not be studied in isolation but in the broader context of sustainable development.

## REFERENCES

Honkatukia, O. (2002), "A Stocktaking of OECD Work on Subsidies", paper presented to the OECD Workshop on Environmentally Harmful Subsidies, 7-8 November, Paris, www.oecd.org/agr/ehsw.

OECD (1998), *Improving the Environment through Reducing Subsidies, Part I: Summary and Conclusions*, Paris.

# Annex A.

## List of papers presented at the workshop[1]

*Session 1.*

*Environmentally harmful subsidies: barriers to sustainable development*
David Pearce, University College London and Imperial College London, UK

*Session 2.1*

*OECD Work on defining and measuring subsidies in agriculture*
Luis Portugal, OECD, Directorate for Agriculture, Food and Fisheries

*OECD work on defining and measuring subsidies in industry*
Frank Lee, OECD, Directorate for Science, Technology and Industry

*The Environmental Impact Of Transport Subsidies*
Chris Nash (University of Leeds, UK), Peter Bickel and Rainer Friedrich (University of Stuttgart, Germany), Heike Link and Louise Stewart (DIW, Berlin, Germany)

*IEA work on defining and measuring environmentally harmful subsidies in the energy sector*
Kristi Varangu, IEA, Energy and Environment Division

*Subsidies and the environment: an overview of the state of knowledge*
(also available in French)
Gareth Porter, Independent Consultant, United States

*OECD work on defining and measuring subsidies in fisheries*
Anthony Cox, OECD, Directorate of Food, Agriculture and Fisheries

*Water-related subsidies in agriculture: environmental and equity consequences*
Mona Sur, Dina Umali-Deininger and Ariel Dinar, World Bank, United States

*A stocktaking of OECD work on subsidies*
Outi Honkatukia, OECD private Office of the Secretary-General

---

1.        These papers are available online at www.oecd.org/agr/ehsw.

*Session 2.2.*

Subsidy measurement and classification: developing a common framework
Ronald Steenblik, OECD Trade Directorate

*Session 3.1.*

*What makes a subsidy environmentally harmful: developing a checklist based on the conditionality of subsidies*
Jan Pieters, Ministry of Housing, Spatial Planning and the Environment, The Netherlands

*Annex B.*

# LIST OF PARTICIPANTS

**Chairman**
**Mr. Robin WILSON**
Former Head of Environmental Economics
Environment Ministry, United Kingdom
Email : robinwilson42@yahoo.co.uk

**DELEGATIONS**

**Australia**
**Mr. Richard SISSON**
Minister-Counsellor (Agriculture)
Permanent Delegation to OECD
Email : richard.sisson@dfat.gov.au

**Austria**
**Ms. Ulrike ETEME**
Federal Ministry for Agriculture, Forestry,
Environment and Water Management
Email : ulrike.eteme@bmlfuw.gv.at

**Mr. Josef BEHOFSICS**
Attaché Environnement
Permanent Delegation to OECD
Email : josef.behofsics@bka.gv.at

**Belgium**
**Mr. Grégoire CUVELIER**
Conseiller
Permanent Delegation to OECD
Email : belocde@wanadoo.fr

**Mr. Frank DUHAMEL**
Secrétaire d'Ambassade
Permanent Delegation to OECD
Email : belocde@wanadoo.fr

**Canada**
**Mr. Adam McLEOD**
Environmental Analyst
Agriculture and Agri-Food
Email mcleoda@agr.gc.ca

**Mr. Stuart CARR**
Counsellor
Permanent Delegation to OECD

**Czech Republic**
**Mrs. Martina MOTLOVA**
Counsellor
Permanent Delegation to OECD
Email : czedeleg005@olis.oecd.org

**Mr. Miroslav HAJEK**
Ministry of Environment
Environmental Economy Department
Email : hajek_miroslav@env.cz

**Germany**
**Mr. Klaus-Jochen GÜHLCKE**
Counsellor
Permanent Delegation to OECD
Email : klaus.guehlcke@germany-oecd.org

**Mr. Stefan BESSER**
Deputy Head of Division
Federal Ministry for the Environment,
Nature Conservation and Nuclear Safety
Email : Stefan.Besser@bmu.bund.de

**Mr. Tilmann RAVE**
Scientific Expert
Institute for Economic Resaerch
Email : rave@ifo.de

**Finland**
**Ms. Elina NIKKOLA**
Senior Advisor
Ministry of Agriculture and Forestry
Email : elina.nikkola@mmm.fi

**Ms. Carita PUTKONEN**
Financial Counsellor
Ministry of Finance, Economics Department
Email : carita.putkonen@vm.fi

**France**
**M. Jean-Pierre DUBOIS**
Conseiller Economique
Permanent Delegation to OECD
Email : sv010-1@dial.oleane.com

**Mme Nicole DISPA**
MINEFI
DREE - 6ème Sous-Direction
Email : nicole.dispa@dree.finances.gouv.fr

**M. Jean KOECHLIN**
De l'Institut du développement durable et des
relations internationales (IDDRI)
Email : koechlin@iddri.org

**Greece**
**Mr. Ilias MAVROIDIS**
Expert, Ministry for the Environment, Physical
Planning and Public Works
International Relations and EU Affairs
Email : deu@minenv.gr

**Hungary**
**Mr. György FEHÉR**
Deputy Permanent Representative
Permanent Delegation to OECD
Email : gyorgy.feher@delhongrie-ocde.fr

**Ireland**
**Mr. Séamus O'FLAHERTY**
First Secretary, Agricultural Affairs
Permanent Delegation to OECD
Email : seamus.oflaherty@iveagh.irlgov.ie

**Mr. Timo PARKKINEN**
Senior Economic Adviser
Ministry of the Environment
Email : timo.parkkinen@ymparisto.fi

**Julien HANOTEAU**
Institut d'Etudes Politiques
Email : julien.hanoteau@sciences-po.fr

**M. Emmanuel CAICEDO**
Chargé d'études au Bureau Synthèses des
politiques environnementales
Ministère de l'écologie et du développement
durable

**M. Jean-Jacques BECKER**
Chef du Bureau, Agriculture et
Environnement
Ministère de l'Economie, des finances et de
l'industrie
Email : jean-jaques.becker@dp.finances.gouv.fr

**Mr. Andreas VAROTSOS**
First Secretary
Permanent Delegation
Email : a.varotsos@greece-oecd.org

**Iceland**
**Mr. Thórdur GUDMUNDSSON**
Deputy Permanent Representative
Permanent Delegation to OECD
Email :
thordur.ingvi.gudmundsson@utn.stjr.is

## Italy

**Mr. Daniele AGOSTINI**
Climate Change Expert
Ministry for the Environment and Territory
Email : daniele_agost@yahoo.it

**Ms. Silvia FRANCESCON**
Ministry for the Environment
Department for Global Environment
Email : francescon.silvia@minambiente.it

**Mr. Alberto BERTONI**
Conseiller
Permanent Delegation to OECD
Email : bertoni@rappocse.org

## Korea

**Mr. Byungkook CHOI**
Deputy Director
Ministry of Agriculture and Forestry
Email : cbk@maf.go.kr

**Dong-Jin YOON**
Deputy Director
Ministry of Agriculture and Forestry
Email: ydj@maf.go.kr

**M. Kyung-Tae OH**
First Secretary
Permanent Delegation to OECD
Email : ktoh@club-internet.fr

**Mr. Tong-Q-Lee**
Second Secretary
Permanent Delegation to OECD
Email : tq.lee96@maf.go.kr

## Mexico

**Ms. Veronique DELI**
Environmental Permanent Representative
Permanent Delegation to OECD
Email : veronique.deli@online.fr

## New Zealand

**Ms. Dawn BENNET**
Second Secretary
Permanent Delegation to OECD
Email : dawn.bennet@mfat.govt.nz

**Mr. Roger LINCOLN**
Ministry of Agriculture and Forestry
International Policy
Email : lincolnr@maf.govt.nz

**Mr. Mark SINCLAIR**
Deputy Permanent Representative
New Zealand Permanent Mission to the WTO
Email: mark.sinclair@mfat.govt.nz

## Netherlands

**Mr. Philip DE WAAL**
Counsellor
Permanent Delegation to OECD
Email : philip-de.waal@minbuza.nl

**Dr. Ronald E. Weenink**
Policy Advisor, Ministry of Housing,
Physical Planning and the Environment
Directorate-General for Environmental
Protection/
Email : Ronald.Weenink@minvrom.nl

**Ms. Pascale Johanna Cyriel VAN DUIJSE**
Policy Advisor, Ministry of Housing,
Directorate-General for Environmental
Protection
Directorate for Strategy and Policy Affairs
Email : Pascale.vanduijse@minvrom.nl

## Norway

Mr. Frode KARLSEN
Deputy Director General
Ministry of Finance
Email : frode.karlsen@finans.dep.no

Mr. Frode LYSSANDTRAE
Advisor
Ministry of Agriculture
Email : frode.lyssandtra@ld.dep.no

## Slovak Republic

**Ms. Martina BRODOVA**
Research Institute for Agriculture and Food Economics
Email : brodova@vuepp.sk

**Mr. Martin SZENTIVANY**
Second Secretary
Permanent Delegation to OECD
Email : szentivany@oecd-sr.com

## Sweden

**Ms. Elin KRONQVIST**
Desk Officer
Ministry of the Environment
Email                          :
elin.kronqvist@environment.ministry.se

## Switzerland

Mr. David WINIGER
Permanent Delegation to OECD
Email: david.winiger@pao.rep.admin.ch

## United States

**Ms. Mary GORJANCE**
Advisor for Trade Matters
Permanent Delegation to OECD
Email : GorjanceMA@state.gov

**Ms. Marca WEINBERG**
Chief, Resource and Environmental Policy Branch, US Department of Agriculture
Email : weinberg@ers.usda.gov

## European Commission

**Mr. Juan RONCO ZAPATERO**
Administrator
Direction générale de la pêche
Email : juan.ronco@cec.eu.int

**Dr. Manfred ROSENSTOCK**
Directorate-General for Environment
DG Env, Sustainable Development
Email : Manfred.ROSENSTOCK@cec.eu.int

**Mr. Mark HAYDEN**
DG Economic & Financial Affairs
Email : Mark.Hayden@cec.eu.int

**Mr. Melvin KOENINGS**
DG Competition (J70, 4/30)
Email : melvin.koenings@cec.eu.int

## Business and Industry Advisory Committee (BIAC)

**Mr. Douglas WORTH**
Secretary-General
Email: worth@biac.org

**M. Marc MAINDRAULT**
Directeur des Relations Commerciales et Financières Internationales
Mouvement des Entreprises de France (MEDEF)
Email : mmaindrault@medef.fr

**Ms. Hanni ROSENBAUM**
Policy Manager
Email: rosenbaum@biac.org

**Mme Sophie LIGER-TESSIER**
Directeur Adjoint
BIAC et MEDEF
Email: sliger@medef.fr

**Trade Union Advisory Committee (TUAC)**
**Mr. John SVENNINGSEN**
International Adviser
Email : JSV@lo.dk

**Arch. Claudio FALASCA**
Confederazione Generale Italiana del Lavoro

**Mr. Giuseppe D'ERCOLE**
Confederazione Italiana Sindicati Lavoratori
(CISL)
Email : guiseppe_d'ercole@cisl.it

## NGO s

**European Environment Agency**

**Mr. Hans VOS**
Project Manager
Environmental and Economic Integration
Email : hans.vos@eea.eu

**European Forest Institute**
**Ms. Olga ZYRINA**
Research Assistant (Forest Policy)
European Forest Institute
Email : Olga.Zyrina@efi.fi

**IMF**
**Mr. Muthukumara MANI**
IMF
International Monetary Fund
Email : mmani@imf.org

**The World Conservation Union (IUCN)**
**Mr. Nicolas BERTRAND**
The World Conservation Union (IUCN)
Email : nicolas.bertrand@iucn.org

**UNEP**
**Ms. Anja VON MOLTKE**
United Nations Environment Programme
Economics and Trade Branch
International Environment House
Email : anja.moltke@unep.ch

**European Environmental Bureau**

**Mr. Sylvain CHEVASSUS**
European Environmental Bureau
Federation of Environmental Citizens Org.
Email : sylvain.chevassus@eeb.org

**Friends of the Earth**
**Mr. Erich PICA**
Economic Policy Analysis
Friends of the Earth
Email : epica@foe.org

**International Institute for Sustainable**
**Development (IISD)**
**Mr. David BOYER**
International Institute for Sustainable
Development (IISD)
Email : dboyer@iisd.ca

**RIVM**
**Dr. Cees VAN BEERS**
RIVM / TU DELFT
Department of Economics
Email : vanbeers@wtm.tudelft.nl

**FAO**
**Mr. Ulf WIJKSTROM**
Chief
Development Planning Service, Fisheries
Department
Email : ulf.wijkstrom@fao.org

**EXPERTS**
**Mr. Peter BICKEL**
Researcher
University of Stuttgart
Email : Peter.Bickel@ier.uni-stuttgart.de

**Mr. Julien Hanoteau**
Institut d'Etudes Politiques
Email : julien.hanoteau@sciences-po-fr

**Mr. András LAKATOS**
Senior Expert (Trade)
Energy Charter Secretariat
Email : Andras.Lakatos@encharter.org

**M. Jean-Luc NIVARD**
Développement durable
Natexis Capital, Banque
Email : jean-luc.nivard@natexiscapital.fr

**Mr. Ron WIT**
CE Delft
Email : wit@ce.nl

**Mr. Marek GIERGICZNY**
Warsaw University
Department of Economics
Email : mgierg@go2.pl

**Ms. Anne HARRISON**
Indepedent Expert
Email : anne.harrison@wanadoo.fr

**Mr. Trevor MORGAN**
Director
MENECON Consulting
Email : trevor.morgan@online.fr

**Mr. Gérard VIATTE**
Email : gerard.viatte@ubiquando.com

**SPEAKERS**
**Mr. Jan PIETERS**
Senior Economic Advisor
Ministry of Housing, Spatial Planning and the
Environment
Email : jan.pieters@minvrom.nl

**Mr. Anton MEISTER**
Professor, Resource and Environmental
Economics, Massey University
Email : a.meister@massey.ac.nz

**Prof. David PEARCE**
CSERGE, University College London
Email : d.pearce@ucl.ac.uk

**Ms. Mona SUR**
Economist - The World Bank
Email : msur@worldbank.org

**Mr. Ariel DINAR**
Lead Economist
World Bank
Email : adinar@worldbank.org

**Mr. Christopher A. NASH**
Professor, Institute for Transport Studies
University of Leeds
Email : cnash@its.leeds.ac.uk

**Dr. Gareth PORTER**
Consultant, Porter Consultants, Inc.
Email : garethporter@erols.com

**DISCUSSANTS**

**Professor Ragnar ARNASON**
University of Iceland
Email : ragnara@hi.is

**Professor Akira HIBIKI**
Senior Researcher
National Institute for Environmental Studies,
Email : hibiki@nies.go.jp

**Professor Gian SAHOTA**
Professor Emeritus
Vanderbilt University
Email : gian.s.sahota@vanderbilt.edu

**Rapporteur**
**M. Michel POTIER**
Consultant, OECD
Email : michel-potier@wanadoo.fr

**Mrs. Aimée T. GONZALES**
Senior Policy Adviser
World Wide Fund International
Email : agonzales@wwfint.org

**Mr. Doug KOPLOW**
Earth Track, Inc.
Email : DKoplow@earthtrack.net

**Dr. Ron SANDREY**
Economic Research Coordinator
Economics Division
Email : ron.sandrey@mfat.govt.nz

**Editor**
**Mr. Michael TINGAY**
Email : mt.11@wanadoo.fr

## SECRETARIAT OCDE / OECD SECRETARIAT

**Food, Agriculture and Fisheries Directorate**

| | |
|---|---|
| Stefan TANGERMANN, *Director* | E-mail: stefan.tangermann@oecd.org |
| Ken ASH, *Deputy Director* | E-mail: ken.ash@oecd.org |
| Wilfrid LEGG, *Head of Policies and Environment Division* | E-mail: wilfrid.legg@oecd.org |
| Luis PORTUGAL, *Senior Analyst, Policies and Environment Division* | E-mail: luis.portugal@oecd.org |
| Carl-Christian SCHMIDT, *Head of Fisheries Division* | E-mail: carl-christian.schmidt@oecd.org |
| Anthony COX, *Senior Analyst, Fisheries Division* | E-mail: anthony.cox@oecd.org |
| Ingmar JÜRGENS, Consultant, *Policies and Environment Division* | E-mail: ingmar.jurgens@oecd.org |
| Dimitris DIAKOSAVVAS, *Senior Analyst, Policies and Environment Division* | E-mail: dimitris.diakosavvas@oecd.org |
| Jane KYNASTON, *Conference Organiser* | E-mail: jane.kynaston@oecd.org |
| Laetitia REILLE, *Principal Statistical Assistant, Fisheries Division* | E-mail: laetitia.reille@oecd.org |

**Environment Directorate**

| | |
|---|---|
| Kenneth RUFFING, *Acting Director* | E-mail: kenneth.ruffing@oecd.org |
| Jean-Philippe BARDE, *Head of National Policies Division* | E-mail: jean-philippe.barde@oecd.org |
| Pascale SCAPPECHI, *Consultant, National Policies Division* | E-mail: pascale.scappechi@oecd.org |
| Julien LABONNE, *Trainee, National Policies Division* | E-mail: julien.labonne@oecd.org |
| Nils Axel BRAATHEN, *Principle Administrator, National Policies Division* | E-mail: nils-axel.braathen@oecd.org |
| Philip BAGNOLI, *Principle Administrator, Global and Structural Policies Division* | E-mail: philip.bagnoli@oecd.org |

Jeanne RICHARDS, *Administrator, Environmental Health and Safety Division* — E-mail: jeanne.richards@oecd.org

Helen MOUNTFORD, *Counsellor, ENV* — E-mail: helen.mountford@oecd.org

Peter WIEDERKEHR , *Administrator, National Policies Division* — E-mail: peter.wiederkehr@oecd.org

Nadia CAID, *Administrator, National Policies Division* — E-mail: nadia.caid@oecd.org

## Trade Directorate

Dale ANDREW, *Head, Trade Policy Linkages Division* — E-mail: dale.andrew@oecd.org

Ronald STEENBLIK, *Senior Trade Policy Analyst, Trade Policy Linkages Division* — E-mail: ronald.steenblik@oecd.org

## Publications

Nicholas BRAY, *Head of Division, PAC/COM* — E-mail: nicolas.bray@oecd.org

## International Energy Agency (IEA)

Kristi VARANGU, *Office of Long Term Co-operation and Policy Analysis* — E-mail: Kristi.Varangu@iea.org

## European Conference of Ministers of Transport (ECMT)

Stephan PERKINS, *Principle Administrator, Transport Policy* — E-mail: stephen.perkins@oecd.org

Andreas KOPP, CEM/DRE — E-mail: andreas.kopp@oecd.org

## Development, Co-operation Directorate

Georg CASPARY, *Administrator* — E-mail: georg.caspary@oecd.org

## Directorate for Financial, Fiscal and Enterprise Affairs

Christopher HEADY, *Head of Tax Policy and Statistics Division* — E-mail: christopher.heady@oecd.org

## Directorate for Science, Technology and Industry

Frank LEE, *Principle Administrator, Industry Division* — E-mail: frank.lee@oecd.org

## Office of the Secretary-General

Berglind ÁSGEIRSDÓTTIR, *Deputy Secretary-General* — E-mail: berglind.asgeirsdottir@oecd.org

Simon UPTON, *Chair, Round Table on Sustainable Development* — E-mail: simon.upton@oecd.org

Vangelis VITALIS *Chief Advisor* — E-mail: vangelis.vitalis@oecd.org

Outi HONKATUKIA, *Principal Administrator, Private Office of the Secretary-General* — E-mail: outi.honkatukia@oecd.org

OECD PUBLICATIONS, 2, rue André-Pascal, 75775 PARIS CEDEX 16
PRINTED IN FRANCE
(51 2003 12 1 P) ISBN 92-64-10447-X – No.53199 2003